the shell and the octopus

the shell
and the
octopus

a memoir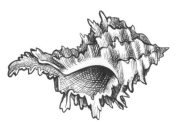

REBECCA STIRLING

SHE WRITES PRESS

Published 2022
Printed in the United States of America
Print ISBN: 978-1-64742-323-0
E-ISBN: 978-1-64742-322-3
Library of Congress Control Number: 2022900128

For information, address:
She Writes Press
1569 Solano Ave #546
Berkeley, CA 94707

She Writes Press is a division of SparkPoint Studio, LLC.

Interior design by Tabitha Lahr
Interior photos are from author's personal archives.

All company and/or product names may be trade names, logos, trademarks, and/or registered trademarks and are the property of their respective owners.

Names and identifying characteristics have been changed to protect the privacy of certain individuals.

I would like to dedicate this book to my family, blood and extended. Thanks to my dad, for his zest for life and for giving me a beautiful adventure. Thanks to my mom, for her grace and support through it all. Thank you to all who have journeyed by my side and shared your experiences in this life with me. Specifically to my dear friend Katie Lawlor, for reading this, supporting me, and giving me invaluable advice. In Montana, thank you to Angela Marie Patnode, who taught me to dive deep, and to Molly Caro May, who helped me play with and evolve my story. In Kauai, thank you to Preeta Carlson, for introducing me to the importance of healing voice, and to Bettina Maurinjian, who guided me, as she has guided so many, through empowering voice. Thank you to Robin Gadient, for the magically held space of her writing workshops and her spirit. Thank you to all who share their stories and support those who need to. And a special thank-you to She Writes Press and Ingram Publisher Services for giving me the opportunity to share our story.

Becky on *Cattle Creek*, Manilla 1972

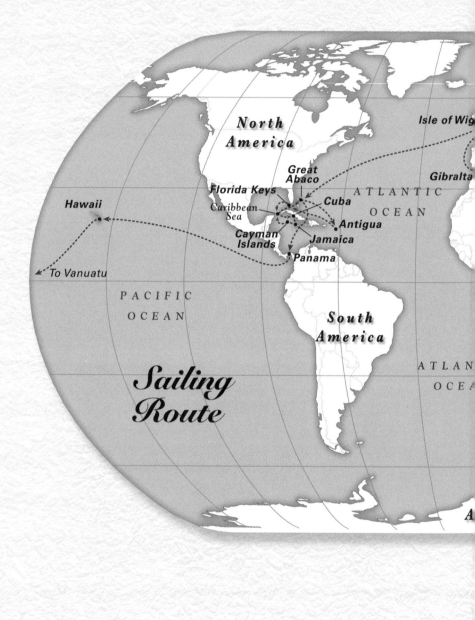

contents

PART III

part I

chapter one

accident

~~~~~~

My eyes flutter open to the blackness inside the boat where I can hear only the waves rushing against her hull. I lift my head to see the orb of the hanging flashlight as it swirls in figure eights over the chart table. The light circles over the teak wood planks of the companionway floor and the teak table where Dad has placed my cup of tea in its wooden holder, and I know it is time to go above decks. I use arms to lift my body off of my bunk because the boat's hull is at an impossible angle for standing, but my bare feet still gain purchase. Wet weather gear feels hot and sticky on my skin as I dress and go out into the fresh, salty night air. This is routine in my half sleep: Brace legs against cockpit and feel blindly into darkness to hook my harness into the lifelines; find the tiller in my hands and see in the compass glow our heading, now 280 degrees NW; and feel for her, the *Cattle Creek*, to give me her direction.

Cattle Creek. It is a funny name for a boat. Dad built two houses in Cattle Creek, Colorado, in the valley named for the creek that comes down from the ranch lands on the plateaus above. He sold those houses, his first in Colorado, and used the proceeds to build our boat.

The silence between Dad and me on this little boat has deepened over the last few days. Day twenty or twenty-one on the open ocean it must be, as the moon will half fill with light for us again soon. Our throats are dry from disuse, our eyes soft with deepened understanding—for each other, this boat, the sea—but mostly with gratitude.

I wedge myself in our little boat's cockpit to ride the pressure of the ocean. In the first moments of the black, new-moon night, *Cattle Creek* and I communicate most clearly. She shudders until I pull the tiller to align her keel in balance with the movement of the ocean, in balance with the force of countering wind in her sails. I can feel her vibrations. And she is listening to me. I must be singing loudly into the wind as we fly wild over the ocean, though I cannot hear myself. No one can, except the ocean. As the boat trails iridescent streaks of plankton in the sea behind us, the tell-tale ribbons from the sails stream in the wind.

Steering the boat is a dance of push and pull with the waves quartering from behind. I dare not look; they would be monstrous giants. I pray as they lift us, but only look ahead. And I listen to *Cattle Creek*, her tenuous lullaby as she shifts with groans, howls, or silence in our sails. If we sail the way we are now, my heart beats calm, even when the black flow of seawater dumps wet down my back and carries my cushion away. The cushion that in calm holds to rest the sinewed muscles twitching in my back.

The sea licks us. Playing. Rough. And the boat tells me now to pull. She tells me to give way, to listen as the wind whistles through her stays. An angel chorus when I do it how she guides. A shrill scream and violent shudder when we are not in tune.

We fly wild over the ocean and surf down the waves in blackness, blind on a roller coaster with no track. Then *Cattle Creek* instinctively noses back into the horizon. My eyes adjust and distinguish sky through grey clouds, which rip open this night with streaks of jagged lightning. The boat shows me with her bowsprit a star to guide us. Glinting like a wink from the heavens, from the sea, an encouragement from all of the nature around me. A wink from my dad and his trust in me as he sleeps through his shift below.

The night of the phone call, my youngest sister Jeannette and I sit on the wooden floor of Mom's sunroom and scrub the scales from my feet with stones and files. We have a metal bowl filled with warm, foamy water, and Jeannette insists that my feet soak in it. I am visiting Mom in Pennsylvania, here to say goodbye, though I do not yet realize the significance of this farewell. Farewell to Mom, like she said to Dad and the boat—and me—when I was ten, but also to Dad and to love, and to everything I have ever known.

I do not belong here. I do not know where I belong. Sometimes I feel as though it is nowhere. But then something reminds me: I am from everywhere. From the ocean and the boat but also, at this moment, from where Mom has moved, close to her roots in a house with a lawn and fence and big oak trees. This place is where my middle sisters, Emily and Sadie, are embarrassed by my feet. And by the way I dress and act. The callouses on my feet are thick, I agree—from so much time with no need for shoes. I am feeling like a mermaid out of water, parched yet still glistening, this particular evening when the priest calls.

My visit here, to Mom's, is only for a few days. We eat meals at the dining table that belonged to Mom's mom.

We are somehow invited to the country club again, where we feel like outsiders while people play tennis and swim in the pool. One time, on a previous visit, we forget my sister there. We remember her when we count sandwiches for lunch at home. Mom and I drive back to find her standing at the fence, tear marks on her face, her lower lip shaking.

In the evening Mom sits outside in the garden at her teak wood lawn table under an umbrella. The table is the only thing here that feels familiar to me, besides the clouds, because of the smell of the teak wood and because it is outside. Mom drinks her wine here. I look out the window from the sunroom while Jeannette works on my feet and see her wine bottle on the table. I do not see her though, and the sky is turning twilight.

But as we try to civilize my feet, all I can think of is the man I am in love with who has just flown home to Switzerland to prepare the third floor of an old chalet for us, and I can't wait to meet him there. A new adventure. A new home. The home I yearn for. Home to his aqua-colored eyes and how he holds the back of my neck when he tells me he loves me.

Gottfried's parents live on the second floor of this home. They don't speak English, though I can communicate well with them because of how I have been raised. The cows with their embroidered neck straps hung with bells live on the ground level, along with the farm equipment. It all smells of fresh laundry and lemongrass and lavender. The sound of water, thank God, whispers nearby from a river of snowmelt.

I have finally gotten myself away from Dad and the boat, and I am here to say my last goodbyes on my way to the edelweiss-covered mountains, only three days from now, with my newly soft feet. But the phone rings. And I never make it there. I never make it home.

On the boat there is no phone, so every time it rings, my heart startles unnaturally. In the sunroom, on May 10th of 1997, I pick up the receiver. The voice comes cold from the other end: "I am the parish priest of Baker County, Oregon." At first I am confused, but then I know. I had talked to Dad a few nights before on his drive from Colorado to Oregon. He told me about the redheaded woman he had met, how she is so soft, like peach fuzz. "We are calling her Peach Pussy," he tells me. "That's gross, Dad. What about the woman in Oregon you are driving to see? What about Freda, in our cabin in Colorado?"

I look out the window to the empty teak table. My little sister looks at me, on the phone with the priest, and we hear him say through the receiver, "I am looking for Mrs. Stirling." My sister knows there is something wrong too. She and I walk the phone up the stairs, leaving a trail of wet, foamy tracks. I cannot bring myself to open the door to Mom's room, knowing that she is in there with her lover for a late afternoon tryst. Jeannette knocks and opens the door a crack big enough to pass the phone through. Silence. Then a shrill scream. Then a sound of something collapsing.

We push open the door to see her crumpled on the floor. I notice Mom's spine, arcing like a string of pearls. Her legs tuck under her, her face hides in the fold of her arm. Her body tremors with each released wail. I know Dad is dead. I want to reach my hand to her back to comfort her, but it looks translucent, and I fear my hand may sink through and disappear and break what membrane holds her all together. Pain has left her so exposed, like when the beak of an octopus drills into the small, spiraled, delicately layered, calcified swirl that protects the creature inside. I feel her wails, but I am not able to release the cry that is in my own heart. Mom dissolves further away from me as my heart solidifies within a thin, crystalline veil. Fragile like a crust of sugar, but its shell strong enough to not collapse and calcify too quickly. I pick up the phone scattered inches from her hand on the floor and listen.

As the priest speaks, all I can do is remember a time just a year before, when Dad and the boat are still real. The priest's voice turns to that dull hum in my head and my mind fades back to the world I know so well. I am on the boat. I feel my face and hair sweat plastered to the musty, blue terry cloth covering of my bunk. Dad's fifty-five-year-old hand gently shakes my shoulder to wake me for my three-hour sailing shift.

But on the boat he would wake me from this dream, and bring me tea, and we would talk about books we love. On the boat, the phone would not ring like this and clench my heart. I would not have to say goodbye like this to him also.

chapter two

earth angels

~~~~~~~~~~~~~~

The morning sun tries to reach through the sheer shades of my sister's room where I drift to sleep and wake sporadically in the panic of knowing that Dad is no longer alive. The tenuous fabric that I have known has had its centre torn out. Like a black swirling hole in the ocean that Dad has disappeared into and I am at the edge of.

I cannot pull myself out of bed. The air seems black, and the humidity presses down on me like heavy weight. My eyes are swollen and tired. My heart hurts. I feel empty like something is terribly wrong. I make myself grip the bed frame and drop my feet onto the floor and feel the wood with raw soles. For a moment, I fear the ground might not still be there at all. But I make it down the stairs and outside to feel the dirt and grass, to see the sunlight reach through the leaves of the trees. I cannot hear anything except the roaring hum in my head.

There is the round, teak wood table under the Cinzano umbrella, but again, Mom is not there. I don't know where she is, but I know I need to get to the table to sit down before I collapse. I don't know how long I sit there. I feel the skin of my cheeks tighten with the hot breeze as my tears dry, then moisten as they pour down my face again, like dripping wax.

After some time, Mom appears in the chair next to me. She is almost fifty now. Still healthy. Slim and muscular. She keeps herself tan and blond. The sun is high overhead. I hear Enya playing. Mom puts a bottle of white wine on the table, two glasses, and then hands me two white pills as she pours wine into the glass in front of me. "What are these?" I ask. "Valium," she answers. I thought I was done with alcohol and I know the pills are a bad idea, but I swallow them with the golden liquid anyway. And I slide into that false, warm comfort once again.

This part is hard. A FedEx package comes with Dad's belongings from the truck. His Levi jeans, his white Fruit of the Loom T-shirt, his Ray-Ban sunglasses, and his leather wallet. His watch, the one with the warranty to never break, is back too. That watch survived without a scratch when he and his sailing partner, Charlie, one of our greatest family friends, threw it against a brick wall to test its warranty. But now it is broken and scraped and encrusted with white blood cells from the accident. His ski jacket has dried blood caked through it also. The priest said he was sleeping in the passenger seat when the truck was smashed.

Again, the phone rings. It is Thomas, Dad's attorney and friend in Colorado. I am the "executrix" of Dad's estate, he tells me. Dad is a single man, and I am the oldest of his daughters, appointed to piece together the mystery of his treasure map. We have to obtain appraisals of the lands he has purchased over the years through sheriff's auctions, trades, and cash deals. I think of the tree house

we lived in, with its freezing pipes. I think of the dome—
the community gym he built that we used to play in, its
trampoline, hidden in the floor, that we bounced so high
on, the uneven parallel bars, the rings that hung from
the high, high ceiling, and the dark, musty cinderblock
shower that scared us with its shadows and spiderwebs.
I think of our boat. It all clicks . . . he had been teaching
me all along. I know his plan, his philosophy, his meth-
odology, his mother's hand scribed accounting methods.
I just do not know about some of the properties he owns.
Or the number of women he was with, or when. Or the
bills. I have no choice but to drive back to Colorado. I
cannot go home to Gottfried.

We—Mom, my sisters and I, our friends—are all so
wrapped up in our own grief, no one knows what to do.
I feel even more alone. I wonder what is going to get me
through this. My experience, my education? Maybe my
naive trust, or whatever this unknown drive is inside.

chapter three

funeral

~~~~~~~~~~

Driving once meant freedom and adventure. What Dad and his friends raised me to live for. Wind in my hair, hand flying in waves out the window through the resistance of wind, singing at the top of my lungs. Now, I cannot even start the engine. My fingers are white as they grip the steering wheel. My heart races as I imagine how the accident might have been, speeding down a rural highway, lazing off the road in hangover fatigue. An overcorrection of the wheel that sends the truck rolling, crunching metal and flesh. This vision repeats over and over in my mind. Over two thousand miles I must drive alone because no one else can bear to be in a car; it feels like a death sentence.

Then I drive up the hill, in view of the mountains and sagebrush and billowing white clouds, to the gravel driveway of the old ranch land where we have lived on and off, in the old cabin, in the tower house he designed on the back of his Copenhagen tobacco can . . . these homes that we lived in while under construction. And when they were finished and sold, we went to the boat on the ocean. This home I drive to is finished. Just in time for the funeral.

Dad's friends Duncan Colman, Amit, and Charlie stand on the deck of the home. Duncan skied with Dad. They were all friends in Colorado when Dad started building homes. This home, Dad shot a bullet through with his .22, from his bed through the ceiling, to show how sturdy it was. Charlie, too, had been living with Dad when that happened, in the guest part of the house. Charlie, I understand, is why we sailed where we did, and he was on our maiden voyage with me as a toddler. Dad met Amit in Haifa after his journey though the Suez Canal. Amit was working as a banker and Dad walked up to him and asked him to cash an American check. Amit laughed and denied him, but liked his enthusiasm, and their lifelong friendship began. Amit ended up moving from the Middle East to live near us when I was young. He bought me my first pair of earrings and he still is family to me.

The deck is angular, with wrought iron railings. Railings Duncan leans against, his broad square chin angling up towards heaven, maybe in reverence to Dad. His sweatshirt has black Sharpie, self-drawn cartoon caricatures of pig-men: the fascist pigs, with ballooned dialogue declaring themselves as such. Duncan is against anyone, especially corporations and government, taking advantage of individuals, our earth, and limiting freedom.

The motto of all these men I am raised by is to journey to "the land beyond, beyond." A Mecca of sorts. Paradise and freedom, And they all go for it. Duncan was an Olympic ski racer, a little if not certifiably nuts, and one of Dad's greatest friends. There is a story that has given him the nickname "Duncan Duck": He was so excited when he won a ski race that, at the finish line, he plunged his head into a snowbank and started quacking. On our boat we named our first pet, a Philippine duck, after him.

Duncan lives in his old blue pickup truck. The passenger side window is missing its glass and is duct-taped and covered with plastic. His truck has a camper on the back where he and his dog, Kiki, sleep. Kiki just had puppies. Duncan brings the puppies into the house, into Dad's kitchen, opens up the dishwasher door, and urges the puppies to jump in. Eager muddy feet paw the opening and Duncan nudges their furry bottoms right up into it. Once his intentions become obvious, someone stops him. It could be my mom. I vaguely hear a gentle voice, drifting from a grieving and confused state: "No, Duncan. Don't close the door. The puppies might not survive a bath in there." Watching it all pass in seemingly slow motion, Duncan's idea strikes me as practical. Spray the puppies off a little bit in there. They are pretty muddy after all. And they stink. Just the quick cycle, no detergent. Dad's ex-girlfriend Freda washes her waitressing aprons in there.

From the other side of the house, rowdy conversations drift. Carl Erickson is here. I do not know him as well as I do Charlie and Duncan, nor do I have the same affinity for him. There is the lore of drug dealing and drug doing, and the greed for money and usury linger in his path like no other in our clan. I follow Duncan through the house. He wanders like a bear ambling his way from one side of the house to the other; it distracts me from the fact that Dad is not, and never again will be, there.

Gripping my drink, I watch Dad's attorney and friend, Thomas, who called me in Pennsylvania. The dear, refined man. Such a gentleman with pleated khaki pants. His hair and beard, once blond, are now silvered grey, trimmed neatly. His crisp blue eyes show a sharp-thinking mind. But his cheeks and nose give him away. Over them the skin stretches translucent, revealing webs of purple veins and broken blue capillaries. He walks as if his hips need oiling, shifting one higher than seems necessary, to get one foot in front of the other.

Emma, the closest to me of Dad's girlfriends, comes and puts her arm around me. She has red hair like fire. Blue eyes and big breasts. She lived with us from when I was ten until fifteen. She probably saved my life with the love and attention we shared, and still share. She sings—always bluesy songs. She flirts, loves, and cries. She taught me the capitals of the countries in South America: Asunción, Paraguay; Paramaribo, Suriname. Time living with her was like burrowing through black moist soil on a hot summer day.

Freda, one of Dad's latest girlfriends, comes up next to me and pushes her shoulder into me, seeing my eyes follow another woman, with soft red hair, mingling around the funeral. The woman skirts most people, just watching. She had been with Dad the night before the accident. We had never even heard of her before that. She gave my sister, also with soft red hair, a white silk pillowcase, "to protect your hair when you sleep," she said. When I ask Freda the woman's name, she says, "You mean Peach Pussy? I don't know her name." I do not ask further.

"He was with you longer than any of these, besides Mom," I say to Freda. A few months before the accident, Dad moved her to our cabin down the road. I don't want to talk to her, but it's impossible not to. I remember Dad's description of her: "A hard worker." I think, brash and loud. Maybe quick and funny, keeping Dad on his toes. "Down to earth," he would say. But he also said she needed to go to finishing school. She gets right up close when she has something to say, like now. So you can feel her spittle on your face. A rare breed, Dad said.

We both quiet when Ruby, for whom he had left Freda (no, not Peach Pussy, but the woman he was driving across country to see) walks behind us towards the deck. She came all the way from Oregon. Ruby is a few years older than I am. Soft and mysterious, long blond hair and deep pools of black-brown for eyes. Her cheeks white like pearls but slightly blushed. He loved her. I did not know her. I do not want to. She lives by a river in southern Washington in a house with a dirt floor. She raises stallions and greyhound dogs and young children. She has cherry trees and keeps bees. Later I find poems from her.

Mom leans on the counter where Freda and I sit. Amongst it all, she tries to make sense of his death, of these women. Still beautiful. Still feisty. She takes the torch as his first, or—if you consider the annulment, his second—wife. She lived with him on the boat the longest. The one he had children with. The classy but bereaved, considering the circumstances. The inebriated singing siren wiggles her butt to the music to make us laugh. I get up and go downstairs to the living room. I cannot laugh.

There are photo albums on the living room table. Albums of my childhood in Peng Chau, Hong Kong, with Mom and Dad and Charlie. In Singapore: a three-year-old me sitting on the boom of our boat atop a furled sail. And the Philippines: a photo of Dad and a gaggle of children splashing in the water on a beach . . . children wearing nothing but the biggest smiles I have ever seen, and me with them. And photos of Dad sailing through the Suez Canal as the first sailing vessel after the Six-Day War. The shot of him taking a sun sight off the port of Djibouti with his sextant is one of my favorites. There are photos of Mom in her small red bikini with me, brown on the beach except for a shock of white hair to match the white Seychelle sand. In Greece: I can almost feel the hot breeze and see the dried brown grasses sway. Dad runs and I try to keep up, to the tops of the mounts where gods and goddesses sing. We run up there to the water wells to sing with them. They echo back to us from the deep, dark caverns. We toss wildflowers into the sky to be carried to the ocean below by the wind.

There are photos of Emma in Jamaica; Montego Bay, and Rick's Café—I can still remember. Her flame hair and a preteen me in white cornrow braids with dark tan scalp showing through. On the boat in the Cayman Islands where, instead of learning about something like the Battle of Gettysburg, I learned that the rum trade runs wild, and I learn about my body from a strange woman. Another of Amit, my sisters, and me in Marsh Harbour. These photos. The only evidence of a vague and chaotic childhood. The only tangible evidence of his life. My fingers drift past them, not touching them for fear of ruining them. The memories. Him.

I find myself needing to leave, arm locked with my sister, drifting down the stairs of the deck out into the field of sage and paintbrush. We just walk. Moths still flit. Grasshoppers jump and hum. The clouds drift long white streams in quiet, through the setting sun, as they always do.

When we return to the house the sky is cobalt and shadowy. Wine bottles and cracker bits litter the kitchen counter. Clear glass bottles have toppled over on the counter, broken onto the floor. Cups with limes and cigarette butts decorate the windowsills and lift a sour stench into the air. I find a blanket to cover Duncan, who sleeps with Kiki and her puppies on the couch.

And the photo albums. There are blank white squares on the old yellowed pages where photos had recently been but are now missing. This is what makes the tears come. The best of the photos memorializing the sailing are gone. I do not know who took them, but the power of the blow to my heart is irrevocable. Outside now it is dark. Only a ghost of Mount Sopris's peak hovers somewhere high in the night sky. A flash of lightning brightens gold for a moment. He is gone.

chapter four

roots

~~~~~

After the funeral I walk the old wagon roads through the fields down to the home where we used to live. The cabin was built in the early 1900s by settlers to this land. They grew potatoes and hay, and raised pigs and cows. The cabin is now half-owned by Dad's ex-girlfriend, Freda, and we own the other half. I go inside, as the door is open. I see a jar of our sea glass collected from Hong Kong, Manila, Greece, the Seychelles. And a Dutch cookie tin filled with coins from the same places and more. Coins with square holes, intricate flowers, and birds. They do not belong to her. They had nothing to do with her. But she has them. I walk outside and around back to the old outhouse and tackle cabin, the old potato cellar I used to play in.

Roots reach from inside of me, they reach and grab to explore what is near. The green shoots curl around the earthen cellar mound the settlers left behind. Now the cellar sprouts sage and Indian paintbrush on top. I can still crawl through the grey, split four-by-fours that form the dark rectangular entrance into the cellar, where roots could survive through dusted snow and blue-sky winters, and hot-wind-scoured and rain-deprived summers. Inside is now just barren earthen walls. And shade. Beside the cellar is the big wooden shed. The lopsided structure still holds cracked-leather livestock tackle. There are rusted cans filled with sour black oil. A bee swims in circles to eventual stillness.

On the walls are hooks with farm machinery parts fabricated in coils and gears like artwork. On the shelves stand bottles of thick purple, green, and white glass that hold the spirits the workers must have drunk as they rested here after work, in the cool shade. The shed is where I go in my heart of curiosity, of history, the land beyond. I meander for hours then go outside into the blinding light and see the outhouse. I want to sit on the splintered wood bench inside, so I do. The sun still shines through the crescent moon carved in the door, making light on my thigh a tattoo that has never left me. The moon, her shadow and her light, is always with me.

The house, old cabin, and shed are cold. Even in summer. Cool breezes seep through the chinking of the beams. Yet the bathroom in the house is warm, so warm the bees built their hive behind the toilet wall, I remember from when I was small. That is why we used the outhouse in summer. We cut out the plywood behind the toilet to see the beehive, the wax lobes draping and dripping with dark syrupy honey, humming. Moving with legs and wings and work. We also used the outhouse in winter when the water pipes froze.

When I am small, I can hear the hive hum as I stand over the heater vent at night. It blows warm air up my light blue flannel nightgown. The edelweiss-embroidered ribbons flutter up, like the tell-tales on the sails of our little boat. As I stand over the heater, I know we will leave here again soon. To find him. My calloused feet will move from these blue-specked laminate tiles of the bathroom floor to the dirt-caked floor of the potato cellar, where wood planks with rusted nails are scattered. I sometimes step on them in the dark and feel the steel puncture my rough skin, finding the soft fleshy inside, that cries blood mixed with iron oxide. Like on the salt-streaked teak decks of the boat slick with ocean albumen when I stub my toe on a cleat and the whole toe end flaps . . . red blood reaches in streaks on the sloshing decks and I can see the tender white layers of skin inside. The roots reach everywhere.

The small wooden table in the kitchen of this cabin is oval with leaves inserted. This, I remember, is where I learn my left from my right, standing against it, looking out the window it is pushed against. Not port and starboard as was ingrained in me, but left and right. Mom and I sit there often. She takes time that day to draw with me—a ballerina because I am getting good at dance. I am even asked to go to a competition in Utah. We draw a beautiful girl, with a bun and a tutu, on point. I feel proud. Then she draws a squiggly line from the bottom of the tutu to the dance floor . . . a dribble of pee. And I feel shame. I don't think I can make it in Utah.

When Dad lives in this cabin he puts me to bed. I sit cross-legged with my back to him, and he brushes the tangles from my hair. He gives me back rubs and stories. Walks his fingers up my spine: ants, spiders, and spots. His voice carries me. Spots where his fingers press in twos down my spine, spiders where his fingers run all over my back. Scratches and tickles and bedtime stories. Stories of travels, of homes he is designing in his mind, or his out-of-body experiences.

And then he is gone. I want to leave also. Want to leave the empty cabin with a manual meat grinder viced to the counter. Leave the laminate brick tiles that cover the natural wood of the cabin floor.

Most of my life I love to leave. Even one summer of back rubs and bedtime stories, and their fighting, I pack a metal bowl and fill it with fruit, and water so it stays fresh. I cannot stand the fighting and want to run as far from it as I am able. I pack a sarong, a jar of water, my book and a journal, a candle and a lighter, and sling them onto my back. I hold the bowl of water on my head and start, in the waning bluish-grey of cooling summer evening, up the old wagon trail towards the baby juniper tree. There is still red Indian paintbrush, cactus blooming white crepe flowers and spines that no matter how hard I try to avoid, somehow fling up from my heels into my calf or skirt hem.

With a sage branch, I sweep to clear a spot below the juniper tree and spread my sarong. I peel an orange, its citrus spray smells comforting. I watch the evening clouds billow slate grey and flash with lightning. I see the side of Basalt Mountain glow blazing red with its fall bush-oak leaves and the last of the sun. I write in my journal. About yearning. A little girl yearning to harness some stirring power in her heart. My eyes awaken to the clear black sky pinholed with stars. The night air is cold on my skin and I feel alone. I do not want to be so alone. I gather my things and walk back to the cabin.

chapter five

wendy

~~~~~

It has been eleven months since Dad's accident. My sister Emily and I think we are finally ready to visit the boat, his sanctuary, my only consistent home. Think we are going to resurrect her. Maybe even him. We carry a notebook filled with lists. Lists for the boat like oysters, wine, bread, and apples. Electrical wire splicers, rags, disinfectant, and lavender candles.

We fall out of our old red truck outside the boatyard in the Ballard neighborhood of Seattle, Washington, and conspicuously walk through the lot towering with dry-docked boats. The smell of epoxy resin and ocean make me lightheaded with ecstasy. Men in overalls soiled with barnacle scrapings turn their heads as we float through the dockyard. My sister's strawberry blond hair follows her like a gown and her eyes smile with the teal blue of the tropics. We see our little boat bobbing amongst the fishing rigs, the houseboats, the bedraggled vessels tied to the dock. The *Cattle Creek*, named after the housing development our dad sold to have her built. Baby Beans is the name of his next subdivision. He asked me to name it when I was five, and I did, after the dolls I played with on the boat.

We step aboard and she trembles like an old genie waking up after a thousand years. She is another sister to me, and so much a part of me. We unlock the padlock, push back the hatch and pull out the wooden slats. A musty odor of circumnavigation, foreign ports, and sweat kept stale for too long envelop us as we crawl into the little belly below. We take our bearings and my sister finds a list my dad had written on the chart table: batteries, caulk, Wendy, wrench, O-ring. "Wendy," my sister laughs. "Who is Wendy?" I wonder why it does not say Freda, or Ruby, but all I can do is shrug. Then a silence falls over us. My sister puts her hand up to his bookshelf. *The Bhagavad Gita*, P. D. Ouspensky, Albert Camus, James Joyce, Carlos Castaneda, a Bible. . .. She stills herself before she touches anything. I can tell by her eyes she is somewhere else, someplace where and when he still is.

I head back to the fo'c'sle and toss my duffel bag onto my worn, blue terry cloth bunk covers. A poof of mildew mushrooms up. I see the little set of carved wooden drawers at the end of his bunk. I reach for the top drawer and jiggle its latch until it slides open. There is a pair of Ray-Ban sunglasses and his sailing knife tied to a lanyard. Under it, I find an envelope.

My sister sees the envelope and we both sit down on his bunk looking at it until my trembling hands are able to peel open the crackled adhesive. Inside, a folded note reads, "I love you." Inside the folded note lies a nest of wiry blond hair. Short and curly. I look at my sister's wide eyes as both of us explode into uncontrollable laughter. Tears drip from the corners of her eyes, I snort, she tries to talk but can get no words out as she gasps for breath.

"Wendy," I say, recalling the mystery item from his list, another woman he loved.

On the Ballard Docks, we inventory the contents of the boat. "Wow. This is serious survival gear," my sister says. We section off the dock with piles of line, spare anchors, dowels for plugging holes, extra cleats, fuel hoses, winch handles, and vials and vials of morphine. I always knew Dad was out to meet whatever God is face to face, but never until then had the perspective that he might be putting himself, us, out there purely to tempt fate.

I open more of Dad's drawers to see what else I might find. A Tupperware container full of leaking batteries, a little white flag—a surrender flag—wrapped around something. I unroll and unroll until something long and dimpled falls out. I hold it in my hand briefly, then drop it and watch it roll down the narrow wooden teak floor under the table between the bunks. A pink vibrator. A rounded end with little nipples, and a blunt end where batteries insert. The boat rocks with the wake of a passing vessel while we just stare, stone-faced. "Wendy!" my sister finally cheers. Wendy becomes our mascot, lashed to the tiller.

With the evening sea breeze, ships pass and their captains bellow to us with horns. We pry open raw oysters with Dad's knife. We drink out of the old plastic tumblers that had served as our drinking vessels on board, the ones he sometimes peed in when the ocean was too rough or he was too drunk, then rinsed only briefly with sea water before filling them for us.

With the rising sun I am up the mast untangling electrical wires. I connect what I think is the mast light, but my sister calls back "stern light," and the stern light connection turns on the light for the head. But there is always a light that turns on, and that means there will always be a horizon for me to sail to.

chapter six

the legal system

~~~~~~~~~~~~~~~~~~~

I n the courtroom I sit reliving, or reinventing, Dad's accident and wondering how the legal system can do this to people. Something strange is going on: our court case simply tries to obtain funds from the policy insuring his life, which he paid heavily into for years, but we have to sue for it. The strange part lies in who we have to sue. We have to go through a small auto policy in order for Dad's life insurance policy to kick in, which should be easy. But we have to fight for it. Because of politics, and "lifestyle" issues.

And it is not like we want the money for ourselves; we have an inheritance tax bill payable to the IRS in nine months, my sisters and I learn quickly after he dies. First, the lawyers have to be hired, with a retainer fee, to research all his legal documents. He has no business name. This is one of the problems. Everything is in his own name. He is self-employed. Because he does not have businesses, or estate planning, as he was young and invincible, we are hit with the worst-case scenario that others bypass with LLCs and wills and family trusts and loopholes; we are billed the most you could possibly pay. Then, the appraisers must be hired to value the land Dad purchased over the years. It is mostly raw land, with no income at all, but apparently it has increased in value. He does not have much cash in his bank accounts.

At the time, my waitressing jobs bring in a few hundred dollars cash a day, pretty good, I think. My three younger sisters still attend school: Emily her first year of college, Sadie her last year of high school, and the youngest, Jeannette, still in middle school. She lives with my mom, who was receiving alimony. The court freezes all of Dad's accounts.

The will appoints me executrix. It sounds like dominatrix. Or something sneaky and bad. In the courtroom I feel like the kitschy star of one of those reality shows I hear about. TV and reality shows, both of which make me feel uncomfortable because they clash with something in my soul that strives for balance. It seems that from the perspective of the jurors, who are not even allowed to know that the insurance company is involved, the name executrix suits my character perfectly. They think we are trying to sue our family friend, when we are merely trying to get access to Dad's insurance policy, which he paid for. We look like assholes. I hate this system.

You see, in order to get the life insurance policy, we have to sue, personally, the man who was driving the truck when the accident happened. It was an accident. Amit, whom I have known since I was five, whom I love dearly—one of Dad's best friends—he is in the hospital with severe back injuries, mourning Dad's death. We are expected to sue him for reckless driving for something like a hundred and fifty thousand dollars so we can get to the insurance policy, which covers anything over that amount. We were not going to sue him, but Amit encouraged us to. Or else we lose all of Dad's property. Everything he has. Even if we try to sell it in a fire sale no one would pay the money it is appraised for. And it won't sell in nine months. Not in time to pay the tax bill. The tree house is infested with beetles, has no heat, and the plumbing backs up. The gym is, in any regular person's eyes, a cinderblock dome with mold and cobwebs and frozen, broken water pipes. The tower-house cabin is half owned by Freda and we can't sell the other half to someone. Apparently, there is fine print we all missed in the National Surety Co. and Fireman's Fund Insurance Co. policies. Getting the first amount, by suing our close friend, is not going to be easy.

My dad worked on oil rigs in the Gulf of Mexico when he was young. He rode motorcycles and hitched freight trains across the country. He worked in a flour mill in Seattle. He worked briefly in coal mines in Colorado, where he fell in love with the mountains. He bought property out in the middle of nowhere just because it was beautiful. He found acreage in a sheriff's auction because someone could not pay their taxes on it, and bought it for $13,000. That was in the 1960s. The appraiser, in 1997, told the IRS it was worth $1,100,000. It just sat there, looking beautiful. Contrary to what the IRS expected, it did not grow money. Granted it has value, but when we try to sell it there are so many stipulations and strange easements that it is not an easy sale, and won't, at that time, bring in that amount of money, but we are still expected to pay the IRS half that value in nine months.

We find he has other property like that. On some of them he built solar houses and tried to develop communities with open space and community hiking trails, ski lifts, and community learning centers. He was ahead of his time with green building and progressive living. He donated the gym space to a local school so rural kids could get an education. He always paid his taxes. "Deductions are cheating. This is what I make, this is what I owe." Be a steward of the land, he taught us. It is not for you, but for you to take care of and give back with.

In the eyes of the system, the land was left to us, and now we have to sell all of it. Fast. Pay the lawyers and title companies and brokers and appraisers and hopefully have enough to pay our taxes on time so the interest will not begin to accrue. Selling the land becomes a full-time job in itself.

"These young ladies want to sue this man. A friend of the family. Millions of dollars. He runs a sandwich shop. What do you think, ladies and gentlemen of the jury?" They scowl at me, representing my sisters, whom I tell to stay home. I do not want them to have to see the slideshow of the gruesome accident. We never wanted to see it in the first place. When the priest, that night, first describes to me what had happened, I say we don't want pictures. Descriptions were enough. I saw the blood on his ski jacket they sent back. The dried pus on his watch. I knew his skull was crushed. Trying to put emotions aside, I cannot help but think how wrong this all is.

The insurance company hires the prosecutor, who distorts this story. I begin to believe him. How horrible we are to do this. How selfish. I want to scream, "Not us! YOU! The insurance company that says we have a policy redeemable upon death! An accident like this is why he paid you for it!!" But I cannot say that. The judge sits me down in a little room before it all starts and tells me I can mention nothing about the insurance policy or the case will be thrown out.

Weeks of this in court. I cannot sleep and hate myself for being this person, this evil executrix, who is trying to get the insurance policy Dad had set up in case this happened. I can't work and my family has no cash. I hate myself for dredging up all the facts in this courtroom that reveal to me what happened that day, two years ago, when the truck rolled on Interstate 84 outside of Baker City, Oregon. Age fifty-six. The stats on the death certificate are really all I knew, or wanted to know. But now I know every detail.

And then the insurance rep, who the jury does not know is the attorney representing the insurance company, pulls Freda as a witness. "Did Mr. Stirling live in any way that was outside of the norm?" Freda smiles in fond remembrance. "Of course! He sailed the world! He rode motorcycles. He rode his bicycle across the United States." And then the question about drugs. "Well, yes," she answers. "He drank a fair amount. And snorted a line or two here and there." She is so honest. "And there were all of the women," she said a bit more quietly. And the representative looks at the judge, who determines that his normal life expectancy would have been lower anyway because of his reckless lifestyle, so he would not have lived to a healthy old age to receive his life insurance benefit.

But the case gets thrown out anyway. Our attorney unearths a document, some insignificant title to some piece of land. It seems to have no bearing on the case but it had not been produced in discovery. Discovery is where attorneys exchange information to prepare for their charade. This charade had taken two years. So, we settle, still not able to claim most of the full policy he had paid for all those years. With the funds, we improve and sell land. Fast.

Finally, I understand why things happen in our legal system the way they do. The reason people who rip off thousands or millions of innocent people, or destroy a section of our ecosystem forever, go free and unnoticed or just get a slap on the wrist. If the jurors knew we were suing the insurance company, they would want us to get at least the amount of our policy. Maybe even more for all the time and hardship in court. The façade is in place to protect the insurance company's rights. Our society's safety net is based on fear—the thing that holds us back. But Dad jettisoned into the unknown, he tested his limits, so his scaffolding of protection was fragile.

chapter seven

peng chau

～～～～～～

On that visit to the boat with my sister I find a letter from Charlie. It is written on the stationery Mom had so thoughtfully made, with a sketch of the boat on the top right, and is dated March 21, 1974, when Charlie returned to Singapore to sail with our family. Months before, Charlie had been arrested there, and held in Changi Prison, for carrying weapons. He and another friend, Gregg, had been hired to crew on Carl's boat, *Steppenwolf*. Charlie and Gregg had guns onboard to defend themselves because they had been attacked by pirates in the Sulu Sea. But guns are not allowed in Singapore, so Charlie and Gregg were thrown in prison. In the letter, Charlie writes some of the best wisdom I know: "It is strange being back here [in Singapore], where I left less than fond memories. But it really doesn't make any difference because what is past is memories, knowledge gained, and nothing more. The sun's shining brightly, it's a beautiful day and with any kind of luck tomorrow will be the same. What more is there to it?"

Charlie also writes in the letter: "We [my mom–Marie Therese, dad–John, Charlie, and I] had a dream sail from Borneo to Singapore. Took six days to cover 750 miles . . . we had an addition to our crew, a small duckling we named after Duncan, 'Duncan Duck,' which helped keep John and Marie Therese's two-year-old daughter Rebecca, 'Bexter,' entertained . . . from Singapore through the straits between Indonesia and Sumatra then almost due west across the Indian Ocean to the Seychelle Islands. It's approximately 3,400 miles . . . and afterwards, depending on whether the Suez Canal is open or not, on to the Mediterranean . . . if not open it means a trip around the Cape."

Memories are disjointed. Some of them have been ignited, and probably reformed, by letters like this one, by stories and by the many journals that Dad and I have kept. It takes me years to be able to even open them. Even holding them brings tears to my eyes. Memories are brought back by the few photos that remain, like me standing, maybe two feet tall in a blue dress, inside a bamboo fish trap on the white sand beach under the shade of palms and bougainvillea, in Peng Chau. I know we are there in 1972, a year after I am born, and stay more than a year while *Cattle Creek* is built.

Dad chooses Peng Chau for the site of construction because Charlie started his own epic sailing journey there. When Carl Erickson, the thug at the funeral, had enticed Charlie and Gregg to help him sail his new yacht, Steppenwolf, neither of them had a clue about sailing, and they used fake checks, credit cards, and drug money to sail the boat that had been built in the same harbour several years before. These are Charlie's tales, the stories I grow up with, of pirates, women, gun running, and, finally, Changi Prison. In 1974, he has recently been released from Changi and is now on a more wholesome journey, with my dad, my mom, and their toddler: me.

I remember the smells of Peng Chau: the saline on the beach by the fishing nets and the colourful wooden boats, the fiberglass resin and the oil for the teak wood on our boat, and the beer from the bottles that collect on the little outside table where we all sit because it is in the shade. I watch the flies caught in the green and brown glass bottles, seeing that all they have to do is fly up out of the little hole at the top and be free, but instead they circle frantically in the heat and eventually land in the acrid beer left in the bottom, then stop moving and buzzing forever.

Dad and Charlie like to have me try the food. After the beers pile up they gesture to the men in the shanties grilling meat that they are hungry, and a plate of steaming rice and meat is brought to them. "Hey Bexter!" Dad calls. "Come and try some food!" Always eager, I scamper over, dragging my doll, and he lifts chopsticks full of meat into my mouth. One time, the men laugh and slap their knees. "Chow chow! Like chow chow!" Dad had fed me grilled dog meat.

I run myself ragged with kids who speak Cantonese. We have sticks and catch big brown crabs from the rocks. We grab handfuls of rice from the big wooden scoops their moms hold out for us. The sun sets. Then it rises and I wake up on cots in bamboo huts filled with other kids, their moms stirring big pots over hot flaming burners or sitting on mats shelling beans.

Cattle Creek grows. The hull of her belly is painted white like a whale. A blue and yellow stripe is painted around the top. The teak plank that will serve as my perch in our travels is bolted to her bow; the "bowsprit" it is called. I sit there on our sails that are calm, my little legs dangling to crash into the blue cool below, hoping to ride the back of the dolphins spinning there. When the bowsprit is secured by bolts and tightened to the rails, I see *Cattle Creek* come alive. It looks like her nose, above a huge smiling mouth, and her portholes are wide-open, all-seeing eyes. The cowl vents, the oval protruding air vents on top of each side of the cabin, look like a cowl neck sweater pulled over someone's head, or just like little ears. She is my sister, I decide as she smiles at me.

As she is built, one of my jobs is to poke the sawdust out of the scuppers, the little holes at the edge of the deck where the ocean water is supposed to drain out. I do not understand, then, when the boat is on land, how those holes will even come close to water. But I learn.

Mom is happy here. I still nurse a bit at the beginning. Then she finds a yellow plastic bottle for me in one of the little sales carts on the street. I carry that bottle with me everywhere. Mom likes the street carts and the fabrics at the markets, and she dreams about the travels ahead.

Finally, it is the day to embark on our sea journey. From Peng Chau we head towards Manila. The sails go up like angel wings and the land gets smaller on the horizon behind us. The water sounds like a lullaby and rocks us. The sun sets and the sky is golden orange, then blue violet, then black.

This is when I meet the moon. She comes bright in the black night sky like a surprise, illuminating her path to us. She instigates the plankton in our wake and they glow like fairy dust. Ocean creatures swim below and beside us, also leaving trails as if from Tinker Bell's toes. My eyes open wide to her, this moon. She is a gift to me, my treasure. And she gives, through me. If it were not for her guidance, I don't know how I could have survived, raised kids, loved. She lets me know there is always magic and mystery to light our way.

I sit curled in my mom's lap, feeling her tense up and trying to hold still in the cockpit. Mom is quiet. Mesmerized. Uncomfortable. I am in heaven on her soft, warm lap. I am swooned by the gliding of our boat and the moon. The moon. I stare at the moon as she seems to ease back into the sky like a lady, releasing her shawl to drop onto the ocean, trailing sheaths of long threads floating, then saturated and sinking like ether. Her white spirit is submerged under the surface of the ocean, opaque. Large glowing movements dart about under the surface of the water. Some parts of her shawl stay dry. Crisp, white. Flitting in the breeze. And other parts float billowing on the surface of the sea. She trails her shawl in a long line to the horizon, and beyond.

The moon always rests content. Her fingers twirl a star, and her beams ripple slowly with the slight breezes of Earth's orbit. Her eyes gaze moonbeams on lichen and coral and anemone, which bloom and spawn on a special night when she is fully illuminated, but only once a year.

As I lay in Mom's lap and nurse, I look at the moon and feel my eyes heavy. I imagine the moon's eyelashes held in space collecting moisture. A dewdrop glides over her iridescent cheek. I understand then, it is a shooting star becoming stardust on a blade of grass. Sprouting, rooting, and reaching. This is how orchids blossom and seahorses reproduce. This is what invites bees who live in honeyed octagon homes to pollinate our beautiful Earth. As I fall asleep the moon visions linger in my mind's eye, like the octagons the stars make when I squint up in her moonlight through tears.

The morning brings scorching, glaring sun and consistent wind. The water does not show us what is beneath her now, like in the night, but reflects like a blinding mirror. Mom and I begin to feel nauseous. In the distance there is an island, and Dad and Charlie direct us there. The opening of the island will bring us to Manila and is called Limbones Cove.

When we anchor, Dad decides I need to learn how to swim. He prepares to dive in, first tossing an inner tube into the water. I realize the tube is meant for me when he hoists me up and I find myself already sailing through the air towards the water. I hit the water. It feels warm and I sink down slowly. Time seems to stop, and everything becomes quiet and peaceful. Darker as I go deeper, and a little cold, my lungs, my throat, compressed. Somehow, I know not to breathe in, or out. Looking up, I see the clear blue sky, distorted only by my bubbles and the rays of light refracted through the water. And I see faint iridescent glowing in the water. It speaks to me, calms me in my inability to get air. As I feel my small chest begin to tighten and convulse, I suddenly begin to rise. I am shooting to the surface. Dad's hand grabs my arm. When I gasp the oxygen, I am crying seawater tears and I scream my childhood word for protest, "noni, noni, noni!" My breath is raspy and through blurry eyes I can see the long white ribbon of beach backed by a forest of palms. Dad and Charlie laugh as we swim in. The sun is just sinking.

There is a man on the beach who hides behind the sand dunes and watches us. I think later how he must have felt invaded by us. When we emerge, dripping with sea, onto the sandy earth, Dad throws me up on his shoulders and I hear the wind blowing through the palms above us. A monkey lands on my head and starts picking at my scalp. Again, I scream, "noni!" I cling to Dad.

chapter eight

queen of the sulu sea

~~~~~~~~~~~~~~~~~~~~~~~~~~~~~~~~~~~

From Limbones Cove we sail through the Sulu Sea to Borneo. I lay on my bunk, sticking to the blue terry cloth that covers the moldy rubber sleeping pad. In and out of consciousness, I feel my tiny body lull back and forth into awareness. And there is the feeling of the boat charging forward, like a wild, galloping horse. This is my cradle. The ocean sounds like a village tribe throwing bucketfuls of water against the side of our boat, then women of the tribe shaking rain sticks to tempo as the boat heels over and her hull is exposed to the sky and tries to dry . . . slosh. . . chchchch . . . slosh . . . chchchch . . . my lullaby.

I remember cutting through and riding faster than the waves because the wind is high and at our stern. I know the hull on the outside submerges on one side deep into the ocean and the mast tilts about forty-five degrees, then comes up to ninety, leaving the hull to sheet water off as it is momentarily exposed.

It all goes black. When I awake next there is a tight pain in my belly, the muscles wringing from stomach up to throat, bringing up only small drizzles of condensed yellow bile. Mom tries to guide it from my lips to the rim of a sun-cracked Tupperware bowl, my hair soaking up most of it. Her fingers red and glistening, like below her eyes and nose, and her shoulders quaking from hours, maybe days, of this as I drift in and out.

Black again. When I come to, Mom is finally lying on her side, on Dad's bunk, her face sweaty with strands of soft sun-streaked hair. She holds herself in desperate sleep, in a fetal position that rocks rhythmically with the gallop of *Cattle Creek* through the sea. Her forehead gently drums the teak slats on the side of the hull with each surge of wave. Bang, bang . . . I can feel the indent on her forehead. But she is still asleep.

"Bexter Bomber!" I hear his cheer through the companionway and turn my head to see his huge grin and bright blue eyes. His soft dark hair blows wildly and his wet weather gear glows orange like a glistening seal from the constant spray of the ocean. I cannot help but smile . . . then black out again.

When I next awaken I am well enough to play with my pink and yellow Baby Beans dolls. I know I can even sit cross-legged when the boat is stable enough. And I know to be thankful that I am alive. I know the dark spirit has lifted from me, and though my body feels weak and slight and hollow with its absence, I am profoundly aware that it is gone, and I am well.

The longer we are at sea, the more time Charlie stays down below with me. I have my bottle, our Sony cassette player, a Fisher-Price plastic record player, a stuffed Humpty Dumpty egg doll, and two Baby Beans dolls. On the bunks in the cabin, Charlie and I listen to a cassette recording of Sesame Street. "Sunny days, sweepin' the clouds a-way," and in the background Mom and Dad yell at each other above decks. Through the companionway I can see my mom's blond hair whipping in the raging wind, some of it sticking to her face. "When will we . . . miserable out here . . . sick . . . hate you . . . fuck you!" Her voice comes to us in fragments, some disappearing into the wind. I tightly swaddle my yellow Baby Beans doll and give the pink one to Charlie. The dolls smell of mildew from the sea water that moistens everything in the stale heat of the cabin.

Everyone is finally asleep. All at once, which is rare. Mom exhausted from crying and screaming, Dad from his watches, Charlie from trying to stay out of the way, and me from all of it. Duncan Duck is quacking frantically, swimming back and forth between the bunks. Dad drops his sleeping arm off his bunk into water and the little duck scrabbles up his arm to rescue herself, quacking in his ear, waking him. The boat has taken on almost half a meter. The hatches had not been closed and the waves crash over the small boat like it is a toy and fill her. She is sluggish and listing.

Dad sloshes through the water to the bilge and inserts the manual lever to frantically pump. The rest of us scoop water out the hatch with buckets. I use my Tupperware bowl. Duncan Duck shakes herself on the chart table, drying her fuzzy little feathers.

Dad always tells me I can be the queen of the Sulu Sea. What does that mean? Why would he even say that? I only remember glimpses of that passage: being so sick, gazing at the moon, learning how to swim, and knowing that I survived—maybe that is why Dad calls me the queen of the Sulu Sea. I know Charlie journeyed there before he sailed with us. I ask him to tell me about it, this thing that is such a mystery to me yet apparently a big part of my life. He gladly tells me how he dove with the sea roving gypsies who lived there, and about the man who brought him to their floating community. This is where Charlie and his crew bought weapons to defend themselves against the pirates who shot at them.

Charlie tells me he and Dad talked then about how I might have been queen. That we could stay there on the boat, and I could be raised and then have babies with a local man and become queen of the Sulu Sea. But now that name is just another thing that is too high an objective. It feels like when Dad hugged and praised me when he was drunk in the bar. Some disjointed expectation of his that I could never live up to. But it also gives me a feeling of possibility, like the unknown inspiration I might feel in painting or writing, in making love, in holding the small, warm fingers of my children.

Sailing on the frothing, deep-turquoise ocean, we continue to Singapore, where Mom and I coddle Duncan Duck, our fuzzy yellow passenger who has saved our lives. She waddles in the cockpit. And snuggles on my bunk with me when it is time to sleep. We make it to the Seychelles, but when we arrive, Mom and I will have to get off the boat.

chapter nine

seychelles

～～～～～～

I sit cross-legged on the bow of the boat, on top of the piles of billowed sail bags, watching as we move across the glassy water and over the rippled sandy bottom below towards faint land on the horizon. I hold a stick, and my small arm reaches it above my head, topped with a white shock of hair, and I wave it as if I am conducting an orchestra. Dad always has Bach or Mozart blaring.

I throw my yellow bottle overboard and watch it float beside our boat, then behind it, then disappear forever. I start to cry. Charlie looks at me and laughs, so I laugh too.

Across the water as we come into a bay of the Seychelles islands, maybe sixty yards away, is the boat *Sirocco* that we sometimes sail with. Her long lines lay on the water, and her captain stands proudly over her on the aft deck. As we get closer I can see that the captain is deeply tanned, his angular chin covered by a messy dark beard, and he wears nothing—except a thick leather belt draped down on one hip by the weight of a machete that parallels his penis, which looks huge to me. He gestures my dad to a safe place to anchor.

Ducking under shrouds and leaping over shackles on the deck, I run back to the cockpit to stand squarely behind my father, out of sight, but also so I can peek safely around him as I want. He is similarly tanned, and also nude, laughing and yelling something back in his deep thunderous voice.

When the boat is secure, I look around for Mom, but see that she has already left in the dinghy. She had been crying, always wanting to get to land. Dad prepares to dive in because that is the only way to get to land without the dinghy. He tosses the inner tube into the water so after he throws me overboard, he can push me, and our clothes, and whatever else he needs, ashore. I float with him pushing me, towards the beach, still crying "noni, noni, noni."

On the shore, the boy who belongs to the man with the machete belt waits, standing tall. His dark torso arches slightly back, and his small hips barely hold his worn shorts. Other kids stand there too, looking wild. A girl I have seen before stands with long, straggly, sun-bleached hair in her face.

As soon as my toes feel sand, I run up the beach to the crowd of kids, and they all turn to run, too, up over the rocks, through the small fishing village, to a small rugged road that leads up into the forest. Kids run and scream up and down the banks of the road, in and out of trees, grabbing branches, throwing rocks and sticks.

I arrive at the end of the road. I stop suddenly and watch a rock I mistakenly kick with my toe soar down over the cliff, into the churning ocean below. I suddenly feel fear crawl up my back, and slowly turn to see the kids in a line behind me, blocking the road with a human chain they have formed by linking arms, standing on solid legs spread defiantly wide.

A hot prickly sensation washes out from my centre like a wave until it hits my fingertips hot and throbbing. And my feet burn, wanting to move. My chest tight, my stomach sick. In that moment of fear, I lose control of my bladder, my bowels. But somehow, I know I cannot cry, and I find the strength to pick up a stick and raise it high above my head and walk towards them, determined to get though them. I see a small boy with doubt in his eyes and head towards him. He breaks the chain when I get closer. He sees the look on my face and in my eyes and lets go his hand. I see that gap and I run.

I run and reach the bottom of the dirt road, breathless, to find a small stone building to hide behind. It must be there for a spring, as water pours from inside. There is an altar there, and lots of dead leaves on the ground. I hear a crackling sound and smell smoke. I peek behind the other side, where the girl with the straggly hair from the beach crouches with a pack of matches. She strikes another match and blows into the musty pile, looking at me with a mischievous smile. I want to make fire. I help pile sticks and leaves until the flame grows larger. We continue the pile until it stretches across the road and red flames lazily lick across it, smouldering and burning low, igniting in bursts. When we hear the kids yelling from the path, we run.

We run to the beach and squat over the sand, picking up the translucent turquoise pieces of smooth, warm glass that have been rolled through the breaking waves. I can see our boat out of the corner of my eye, floating calmly now closer to shore. And my mom is hauling a sack from the dinghy. Small-framed, she struggles to pull it up the beach, in her red cotton bikini with small white flowers.

She wears a handkerchief over her head and has a sad look on her face.

She looks up at me and I run down towards her. As I get closer she yells something, stoops down to grab her sack of laundry, reaches out towards me, and grabs at my elbow. She seems different now. She drags me up a path to a small washhouse off the beach. It has cement stalls, painted brightly, and is lit by sunlight coming through a window over the sink, and it all smells so clean. She stands me in front of the sink and pulls my shirt over my head, and yanks my shorts down over my feet, struggling to keep me balanced. She shoves the soiled shorts to my nose, as if I am a cat. Now I understand why she is yelling. I am dirty. More laundry. All I can do is look ahead blankly at the blue cement wall as she moves me towards the shower stall. She is still loud until she sees my eyes.

Then it is quiet, and I stand under the cold water as it runs in small rivulets over my dry, dirty skin that smells like dirt and sun, and stench. She is crying now, wiping at my face with the cleaner parts of my shorts. The water stings my toe as it loosens the dried blood that was holding the tip of my big toe on—the toe that I had stubbed on the rock at the end of the road.

When I am clean, she holds out a big, clean cloth and I bury my face in it, into her stomach, as she dries me. Through her soft crying and muttered words, I can also hear him, in the next stall, my dad yelling and laughing as the cold water shocks and cleans him. "Shamataya!" he says. He says this all the time. I later look it up. It means great leader; protector.

Together, we walk to the tavern where the other adults wait. The boy is there—I do not look at him—and a dark, mysterious woman who holds him. I see her watching Dad for too long and smiling. After a while, I curl up on the floor under the table. It is made of tiny pink-speckled rocks and is polished smooth. It is cool as evening approaches.

Dad talks of going through the Red Sea. There has been a war there, and there is concern about our small sailing vessel going through. Mom and I must fly somewhere and meet him on the other side. I hear this, my cheek against the cool floor, Dad's hand reaching down to scratch my head though my tangled hair. The loud conversation, laughing, and the noise of frogs and distant music become garbled, and my head throbs with the cacophony of sounds, the humming, the vibration in my head.

The boy squats under the table to hand me a marble. I take it in my hand and grasp it tight in my fist. It is warm. I believe it is the moon. I fall asleep.

chapter ten

europe

~~~~~~~~~

Dad gets us tickets to Austria, where we wait for him to sail from the Red Sea through the Suez Canal. Here it is safe for us, but it is so cold. There are log cabins, with peaked roofs, small balconies with carved-heart railings. There is snow everywhere. Snow mushrooming the rooftops and lining the trodden paths. Mom pulls me on a little wooden sled to a store. Inside I rub my red hands together for warmth and notice that it feels like home here. There is fresh bread. There are metal shelves with jars of honey and bottles of oil. A smiling woman in an apron, her daughter bustling behind the counter—I watch them and time slows. I want to stay.

Mom dresses me in a red woolen skirt with suspenders embroidered with white flowers. They strap over my shirt and fasten to the skirt with little silver clips. Mom seems distant. She laughs then cries. We do not often leave the small room where we board. She has been sewing a green felt elf costume for me for Seleenwoche, or All Souls'

Week. On this holiday evening, she pulls me on the sled to other wooden chalets for gifts, mostly candy, that I gorge. Each entry is lit by a torch. The windows show the golden warm insides with families smiling around. Outside it is cold. Mom's face is red and streaked with tears. I know she realizes that she cannot be with Dad unless she lives on the boat with me. And she does not like the boat the way Dad likes the boat. There are people singing outside the church down the path.

When Dad comes to meet us, instead of staying, he takes me away in a small car up a windy mountain pass. My stomach churns and heaves warm syrupy remains of caramel onto the elf costume I always wear.

Dad must have taken us back to the boat, moored in Greece. He wakes up early and swims me to the shore; "noni, noni, noni," I cry. White rocks with orange lichen feel hot under my small wet hands. I grasp dry grasses, some with purple flowers blooming in lollipops at the end. Holding yellow Baby Beans under my arm, I swipe at the grasses and flowers and crumple them into a bouquet as I follow Dad, his warm smell of tan and sweat, up the hill. He is crying. His dreams of sailing with his family on the boat do not work. We find deep cavernous cisterns of water and call down to them, to the other side of the world.

Mom waits on a bench at the bottom of the hill. Her legs are crossed with a whispering white gauzy cloth around her waist, her red swimsuit with small white flowers against her tanned skin. She looks calm, almost smiling, but distant. As we arrive she stands and clasps my hand in hers. She smiles at me but does not look at Dad.

We end up in a huge cave with light refracting from the ocean and water at one end, and the sun pouring down through a hole at the other end. It must be some tourist site, as there are a few others with us, all quiet, as we walk slowly, in bare feet, cool mud squishing through our toes. The floor of the cave is convex, and I remember trying not to slip down the subtle sloping sides, where the ocean water laps in, emerald green.

Though Mom and Dad do not talk, and I feel a shift between them, we are all holding hands together and I feel free and curious. I have no fear.

I sit on the floor of our flat with trains of paper egg cartons. We are on the Isle of Wight in England. I might be four. The woman at the harbour had helped us find this place and she also owns a candy store. She gives me bags and bags of sweets and I make trains with the candy, the coloured wrappers, and egg cartons. I play with my candy train until there is nothing left but egg cartons and shiny wrappers, and my stomach and head hurt.

Somehow I end up in school, kindergarten. I wear a grey uniform with iron-on patches. The skirt is knee length with a flat panel in the front and pleats on the side. I fumble with the buttons of the shirt, and the collar folds down. The ironed starch feels rough and scratchy on my skin. I need something that is mine, so I choose my rainbow socks with separate-coloured toes. Red, orange, yellow, green, blue. The headmistress pulls me out of class because I cannot sit still.

chapter eleven

marsh harbour

~~~~~~~~~~~~~~

I must be six now. Memories here are both foggy and clear. What is clear is that I am in Marsh Harbour, the largest town on Great Abaco Island in the Bahamas. We are at Dad's father's house here. It is simple: white concrete walls, metal corrugated roof, and tiled floors. I wander here alone.

In the backyard there is a washing machine with a metal drum that we fill with water, and there are two rollers fastened about two feet above the top. There is an electrical wire snaking from the house, and when I press a button the rollers begin rolling so that I can feed the wet clothing into them and they squeeze out the water. I am the laundry girl, so I experiment. My index and middle fingers that are holding a shirt keep going through the rollers and I cannot pull them out. I scream as I look at my flat and purple fingers.

There is also an old rusted car in the yard. It has pedals, like the Flintstones cartoons. I get in and roll the old rotten coconut out of the way of the pedals so I can get this thing moving. But the coconut is home to a hornet's nest and they swarm me. It is bright light and stinging pain. I ache everywhere and lay in bed under a thick white sheet for days.

I think Mom was in Colorado for a while, maybe because I puked all over the elf costume she made me for Seleenwoche. And I know she hates this boat. Across from the house is the Conch Inn Hotel and Marina. This is where I can find Dad. He orders us fried conch fritters. When we come home to tuck me in and give me a back rub, he tells me my mom loves me.

Mom comes back and somehow I have a little sister, Emily. Dad and Mom need to work things out, so they leave Emily and me. She is in tiny diapers. Amit is also here. I am supposed to stay with Amit, who is trying to figure out how to move to the US. Emily is with Jim and Maria, our friends from Amsterdam. Jim did the sail through the Suez with Dad, and they are now like brothers. Dad tells me he and Jim talk about communism on the boat. And literature.

Maria always has Emily on her hip. She holds her and bounces her and Emily smiles and watches. Amit and Jim tell me that Mom and Dad are sailing to a beautiful nearby island and later we will meet them. They just need to spend some time together because . . . I know why. Because of the yelling. And the way Mom was acting. Crying and mad at everything.

Jim and Maria, Emily, Amit, and I take a quick flight in a tiny plane to meet Mom and Dad, who come to the airport from the boat. There is a huge pane of glass between the people waiting outside and us, the passengers getting off the plane, and all the military people who are at airports. But when we pass by the glass, and Maria hands Emily to Mom, Emily won't let go of Maria. Emily looks at Mom and Dad with terror in her eyes and she screams and clings to Maria. The military guys wonder what is going on and think Mom and Dad are trying to buy a baby.

chapter twelve

colorado mountains

~~~~~~~~~~~~~~~~~

My next memory is being home in our cabin in Colorado. I must be about eight because Mom and Emily and our new baby sister Sadie are there. But Dad is not. I go to a school outside of Aspen with a huge wooden tower that looks kind of like our house. We get to call the teachers by their first names, and we play outside in the ravine. We make forts in the trees and sled down the ravine in the winter.

In the morning, the bus driver and the principal have us stand up and sing songs. Then we go off to learn computer programming, or to build a proportionate-sized planet out of papier mâché. I chose Jupiter, and it takes up the whole room.

But then I was always in trouble, walking with the teacher outside or dumping out all of the garbage cans into the central area to look for something I misplaced. Even though I always felt like I was a bad kid there, I felt really smart. Except for my spelling marks because of what I was taught in the school in the Isle of Wight, and the Charlotte Mason Spelling book mom gave me on the boat. Colours, not colors. And that was how most of what I read and saw, was written, like the signs for the Harbour. And I wrote in journals for all the time that I missed school because of the boat.

chapter thirteen

sleepy cat motel

Dad has been at the bars a lot. Charlie sometimes picks me up from school in his huge Ford truck, his bull-mastiffs barking in the back. Or sometimes I just walk to my friend Mary's house. I have learned to pack a change of clothes, because Mary is tall and skinny and her jeans don't fit me. And she is sick of me borrowing. I pack bread or crackers too. Just in case.

Sometimes Dad takes me on adventures. He takes me on his motorcycle to Harvey Gap, a reservoir a few hours from our home, so he can practice windsurfing. Dad swears as the sail and mast fall on him when there is a lull in the wind. He splashes into the water.

I meet a girl my age there and we pick the white asparagus that I eat because I am hungry. It grows on the muddy shores, just where the cottonwood trees stop and the blue grass gets sparse. We also catch crawdads. We can cook them if we need to eat.

Birdie, the girl, and I paddle across the lake on wind-surf boards. There is a waterfall tumbling through the dry red rocks and sagebrush. Birdie's mom flies across the lake on her windsurfer. Her long hair trails behind her and her smile shines through her wise blue eyes. We eat dinner, which I am grateful for, in their little cabin and we spend the night in cozy little beds with handmade quilts.

One morning Dad's motorcycle is out of the garage, so I think we might go see Birdie and her mom again. His huge, heavy, faded black leather jacket and big black helmet are on the table. There is a small blue-and-red leather jacket and small red helmet for me. He is rigging up something for me to lean back against that he can harness me to on the back seat, in case I fall asleep. "Where are we going?" I ask. "Harvey Gap. Then to the desert," he says. But for some reason we don't really stop at Harvey Gap this time, or see the lady and Birdie. We keep going. Fast.

My helmet is so heavy that my head falls back in resistance to the wind. It hurts my neck to hold it up straight. I try to hold onto his wide leathered back and find the place where the wind can't reach. He winds faster and faster on the old single-lane back roads. I feel like our knees will graze the pavement as he leans in with the turns. It is midmorning and the air feels hot and dry the further north and west we go, down from the mountains into the plains. There is a straightaway and no cars. He accelerates and I feel afraid. We pass an overturned van with charred-black front windows. I begin to cry and yell and pound on his back with my tiny fists. He cannot hear me. He must not feel me. We continue on and I realize all I am doing is exhausting myself.

The trick is to change my mind and distract myself from the situation. This time I stick my tongue out of my mouth for as long as I can count. I feel a bug land on it;

it dries and sluffs off. I hold my tongue out longer. I feel the moisture from inside my lips seeping out, wanting to do its job but failing in the wind, the heat, the dry. My hand reaches up to touch my tongue and it feels like the belly of a snake. Or what an iguana might feel like.

And the rain begins. The light grey of paved road, the almost-white sunlit sagebrush, the yellow goldenrod flowers suddenly have a change of shade, like a colour lens has been placed as a filter before my eyes. Richer, darker, and bringing the smells. The odor of hot tar and dust, the spicy tang of sage, the melting honey of the flowers. And I let go.

He does not slow down, even at the risk of sliding on the wet turns, but only becomes more resolute and solid. So, I fly, relaxed, leaning into the metal backrest he has made and welded on for me, check and tighten my harness, and let my head roll back to feel it catch against the metal. I am so exhausted. I sleep.

It is dark and we are in a small town. I wake up because we are no longer flying at top speed. "Meeker Gas," I see in red neon lights glistening more profoundly in the rain. We are in Meeker, Colorado. There is a park and I can tell he is looking for a place for us to stay. I hope we can stay in a motel since it is raining, but say nothing. The Sleepy Cat Motel and Cabins. He turns left and pulls to a stop, turning the key off. The bike feels strange without its loud vibration and momentum. He leans it over on the kickstand and helps me off. My legs feel wobbly. We walk inside and sit down at a tavern bar and he orders us chicken fried steak and mashed potatoes. There is brown gravy. I am so tired and the warm food in my belly feels so good and makes me groggy.

Our cabin has one metal-framed bed and we both lie down in all of our clothes and fall asleep. He wakes me up in the middle of the night. I am soaked. I have soaked him. It smells of fear and urine. He puts me in the bathtub with my jeans on and leaves some clean clothes and towels for me. I wash and dry the best I can and crawl back to bed, to the dark veils of somewhere else.

chapter fourteen

wild horses

~~~~~~~~~

Felice takes me in. I am ten and have started fifth grade. She is a friend of Dad's, tall and loud and pretty and does not like to stay at the bars as long as all of the guys. Bill, another friend, and Dad spend a lot of time planning some real estate project, something about people not paying their property taxes and the deeds going up for auction. They talk about legal things, and drink a lot of beer. Bill's daughter Greta is in the bars now too, which is fun for me. She is two years older and there is someone for me to play with.

Felice lets us sleep at her house sometimes. We stay up and watch scary movies. We watch *The Exorcist* and it sears into my brain. Linda Blair's head spinning, her white sickly face. I cannot sleep well for weeks. Maybe months. I actually cannot sleep well for years. In the daytime Felice takes us horseback riding.

We go for hours into the Colorado foothills. Through aspen trees. Through the fields and ditches, jumping fences and ravines. We talk about boobs and bras and how they act when riding a horse. And brushing our hair. And the horses' manes. And braids.

The horses have something called frogs in their hoofs—the soft part that you have to clean the mud and pebbles out of. We learn to stand quietly by the horse and gently squeeze the heel so the horse will raise it for you to clean. And we brush. There is the warm, clean smell of sweat, and hair, and something medicinal, like vapor rub.

We clean the stalls, rake the neat clumps of hay-bundled poop into the corner and shovel it into a pile at the back of the barn. At school I sit in the back with all the kids dressed in black and help them get one hundred percent on their quizzes. I know them from the bars. Emma, the girlfriend of Dad's I get along with, starts to visit. She and Felice laugh in the bars, and don't drink as much as everyone else, and they usually leave earlier, and take me with them. I get more sleep. It feels fun.

Greta and I make it to the horse barn one morning before Felice. We clean and prepare the horses. She still does not come, so we put on the bridles and hoist ourselves up by the fence, bareback. We take off in the field by the barn, cantering as fast as we can. I can hear Greta laughing. Then I hear her calling my name. Faintly, and something is wrong. I cannot see her, only her horse grazing, bridle dangling in the tall grass. Finally, I see a long leg stick straight up into the air, and her hand waving. She keeps calling and I turn to get to her. I dismount and see that she is on her back on the ground by a ravine. They tried to jump and the horse fell, rolled onto the ground, Greta's leg underneath.

Felice drives up just then and I run to her, with my horse, her bridle still in my hand, to tell her what happened. She opens the gate and drives through the fields to Greta, tells me to put the horses away and get back to the car. Greta's leg is broken.

chapter fifteen

florida

~~~~~~~

Dad is ready to take to the sea again. To the "land beyond, beyond." He invites Bill and his daughter Greta, full cast and all, to join us on a voyage from Florida through the Caribbean. Greta is thirteen, and I am almost eleven. We all meet in the Florida Keys, where the boat has been for that winter while Dad worked in Colorado and while I went to school. We prepare for our journey to Grand Cayman Island.

March 20, 1982—Journal Entry

We were awakened by Daddy to go to the airport and fly to Tampa, Florida. We woke up at 5 a.m. When we got to the airport, we went through the check-out counter and all that and got on the plane to Denver, then went to the next plane. Then Daddy got busted at the check-out counter because he had a pocket knife they said he had to put in the luggage. So, they did and found the guns Daddy brought for target practice. The stewardess said that he had the FBI waiting for us but they didn't show up and that was a relief.

~~~~~~~~~

Early morning pink clouds hover over the Shell Point Marina in Tampa. The masts sway in discord, more frequently as the sun rises and the motorboat traffic picks up. Greta and I start up the dock, out the gate, and down the long stretch of sidewalk flanking the now-empty road. She has a funny boot on over her cast, and hobbles a bit. We talk of what books we have for the trip. I tell her I have *The Incredible Journey*. She frowns. She tells me about *Are You There God, It's Me, Margaret*, and *Flowers in the Attic*. I nod as if I have heard of them. "What else should we buy?" I ask, thinking of gum, maybe sneaking some candy. Greta lists "razors and cigarettes." I feel small next to her.

We find a store after an hour of walking. I am thankful that when we get to the aisle with one-pound bags of Hubba Bubba bubble gum, she is just as excited as I am. I throw two bags into the basket. She throws in Camel Lights, a lighter, and a pink Gillette razor, all of which excite and scare me. I grab Tic Tacs for the cigarettes.

Our walk home is much longer because the sun is up and blazing and Greta's leg is sore. That night our calves burn with pink, sun-fried flesh that stings against the terry cloth on our bunks.

April 13, 1982—Journal Entry

Today we finally started off sailing. First Greta and I ate a whole bunch of gum (we bought 132 pieces each). Then we had ravioli for lunch, it was gross. Greta and I were telling each other what we would do if a tidal wave came. Then we had spaghetti for dinner. Dad and I stayed up and looked at the stars.

chapter sixteen

cuba

~~~~~~~

On the sail to Grand Cayman, we are sidetracked in Cuba. We try to skirt Cuba, leaving it to our port side. Cuba/US relations at the time are highly strained through the aftermath of the Cold War, the Bay of Pigs, with continued tension between the Reagan administration and Castro.

~~~~~~~

On the white sheets, once pressed and starched, there is a large red stain in the shape of a hibiscus flower. The top sheet is piled on itself, starkly exposing the flowerlike pattern against the white of the sheets, the white hotel room. It is the room Dad shares with Bill. I take notice of the blotch and file it away in my head, like so many other things. It can't bother me. Just like I cannot let myself be concerned with the armed guard posted at the hotel room door. I have to pee.

The guard at the door tries to dissuade me from going inside, I know by the nudge of the rifle in my direction, but he also sees my urgency. We do not know the same language. Neither of us knows what to do other than these are the only toilets I can use, so I just push the door open further and walk in.

The bathroom door in Dad's room is closed, so I go into the adjoining room I share with Greta to use the toilet. Finished, I start out towards the guard. I walk out through Dad's room and notice his bathroom door is now open. Then I see long dark hair, and a pant leg of blue sateen, wisping over a high heel. The blood on the sheets is hers.

~~~~~~~~~

The tropical storm on our route to Cayman ramps up to a full gale and the boat is heeled over so that the leeward deck is submerged in water, pouring out the scuppers when they see air. We all hook into the lifelines and hold on, through whipping, soaking winds, our knuckles white and bleeding. Bill's feet are so sunburned that they have blown up like a puffer fish and he can only try to support himself with his straining arms. Greta is down below, rolling between the leeboard and the hull of the boat on her hot sweaty bunk, moaning as the cast of her broken leg bangs with each heaving pitch of the boat. I lie in my bunk, trying to read. I find a spot between my legs that makes me feel good, calm, in another world. But then I feel nauseous again, so I scramble above decks. I puke, aiming for my bucket, but the wind just carries it, wide ribbons of yellow bile dancing with my hair and splashing the deck, along with the rain and sea water. Dad uses these happenings to justify easing closer to Cuba, into calmer waters. He uses them to justify an adventure in Cuba.

"What the hell," Dad says. "Bill—from a legal standpoint, what's the worst that can happen?" Bill just grunts, miserably. I dry-heave again, Greta moans. Dad, out on deck, grins wistfully at the sea. I hear his menacing laugh in the shrieks of the storm, which means, I know, that he is going to bring us to Cuba. Illegal for Americans at the time.

Once we cross the invisible line into Cuban waters, a faint dot comes towards us from the hazed outline of land that is emerging through the now land-sheltered gale. The dot grows quickly, and we realize it is a boat filled with men in army fatigues, carrying machine guns.

Not only are we in Cuba, but we are under arrest in Cuba. "Manos detrás de la cabeza!" A square-jawed, dark-eyed soldier shouts for us to put our hands behind our heads. He yells from the speedboat as it encounters *Cattle Creek* and they grab onto our deck rails, our boats clashing together in the thrashing water. Realizing we do not understand the command to put our hands behind our heads, the man looks at my dad with piercing eyes, and waves his crew to board the boat. Sitting on the aft bench, Dad folds both of his hands behind his head in a posture of surrender. "Tiene armas? Pistolas?" he yells. Dad shakes his head. A soldier eyes Bill and me, his gun nudging at my belly. A second man directs his gun to Dad's side, and presses the muzzle in. I imagine blood on Dad's worn T-shirt where the tip of the gun pulls the fabric together, with the muscled skin underneath. The third, the lead commando, sits face to face with Dad, who boldly takes his hand from behind his head and gestures for the man to search the boat. The man nods in acceptance, and clumsily goes below. The boat jostles in the water, clanging awkwardly from not being steered. The ocean feels thick. There is commotion below. Greta makes a short shrieking noise.

Eventually, Dad tentatively lowers his hands from his head, with one hand in front as if to say "stop," and the other, two fingers on the barrel, moves the gun from his ribs. All the while he looks his guard in the eye. "Regga," Dad says, quietly. This is a term he had picked up sailing somewhere; I had heard it like I heard his breath, and now I guessed he learned it in the Middle East, in the Red Sea. Dad says it, "regga," like a purr, with a wry smile, and opens his palms at chest height, repeatedly, slowly pressing down onto the heavy air in front of him. He looks at me and nods, making a motion of chewing. I get up and go through the companionway down the stairs and grab our bag of gum from our, I thought hidden, stash below. It is soft and sticky and the wrapped pieces have leaked a pink goo into the corner of the big bag. I open it and fish out the driest pieces I can, and come back above decks to look at Dad. He nods at me and then to each man. I hold the wrapped chunks of gum in my hand and hand them to each one. They look then take a piece, unwrap it, and chew. The leader closes his eyes for longer than a blink as his jaw moves pleasurably.

My eyes fix on Dad this whole time, for signs, for direction. We understand each other intuitively. This is most painful when I have not met his standards. At times I can feel his disgust with me. But now, I feel his praise. I sit back in my corner and resume watching, amazed, but not surprised, to see his communication immediately disarm our captors. I feel like I have done good. Though my gut is tight with anger towards him and my head begins that pounding again.

"OK!" the leader yells, coming up from below. I look down to see Greta is still in her bunk, untouched, though probably terrified. The soldier gives a nod to his companions. He then gestures for Dad to steer the boat towards land. I know from the chart we are headed towards a small port on the southern part of the island. I feel cold and eerie quiet, despite the warmth and noise of the sea.

The land gets closer. Dad sits with the soldiers around the cockpit. He is talking somehow neither English nor Spanish, one hand gesticulating, one hand gripped to the tiller. The sails are up but Dad has turned on the engine too, for any speed this slow boat can gain. The engine roars and spills out diesel fumes which keep my belly queasy. Greta, Bill, and I are huddled together, sitting in the cabin. Dad hands the men cigarettes, after he lights them for them, expertly in the wind, somehow lighting the match and shielding the flame with one hand.

They sit in a bonded silence, looking toward the ever-closer looming land, as they pull smoke into their lungs. Then finally, breaking this bizarre silence, "Cerveza?" Dad says, with a smile. It may have been his only word of Spanish. It is not clear if he is asking or offering. The square-jawed man replies: "Si. Cerveza. En el puerto. Y mujeras!" He takes a hand off his gun to gesture towards the land, with invitation. He has a wistful smile on his face. Then, seeing that he has been taken off guard, he pushes the tip of his gun towards the tiller and takes a deep pull of his cigarette. With a nod, Dad takes the tiller and puts a stern look on his face, sailing on, towards Cuba. The other men laugh, and take deep drags, blowing smoke out nostrils, or down their chins, before regaining composure.

I watch Dad allure these men, with awe. On the three-hour sail to port, the soldiers are challenged to prove the wonders of Cuba to Dad, without a common spoken language.

In a small, nearly empty harbor, our crew is placed under boat arrest. But, they bring us fresh bread and cerveza daily. The soldiers are invited to climb up the mast and dive off with Dad. We often have laughing visitors, stopping their little wooden boats to peer onto our boat. And soldiers at the dock who watch us have lowered their guns, and they and Dad cheer or yell something in laughter across the water to where we are anchored. "Visa?" Dad asks after the fifth day.

We are invited to climb off *Cattle Creek* into a metal boat with a motor. It takes us to the dock where a small black car awaits us. The driver speaks a little English and we drive along a one-way road. I see small, square plots of land, then we get to a small, grey, fairy-tale-like city.

We are brought to a cigar factory. A man has a cigarette hanging onto his lip and stares straight ahead with glazed-over eyes. His hand is like leather and rolls tobacco, that his other hand expertly measures out, into a huge brown leaf. Then he picks up the finished roll, twists both ends, and places it in a wooden box.

Then the driver takes us to a baseball game. We see the last inning. It is like we are in a movie set back in time. Even the colours seem muted. As we walk out a man brings us the baseball, signed with all the players' names. I love the faces, the smells, the buildings. I want to see inside the houses. See the moms, the families. We then visit a hotel with a Spanish-tiled courtyard and a small restaurant. There are white-painted metal chairs and tables, and a parrot in a cage. Dad, Bill, Greta, and I sit down, in a daze at all that has happened. There are young girls dressed to the hilt parading around what looks like a pool at the far end of the courtyard. Bill looks questioningly at our "escort" guard at the next table. The guard, with an appreciative nod towards the girls, replies, "Fiesta de Quinceañera."

I notice a beautiful girl in the parade. She is taller than the rest and has a small waist, and is wearing a silky blue bodysuit that curves gently over her hips, down her long legs, flaring out into bell-bottoms that flow over strapped-on high heels. I blush as I follow the fabric that crosses over her young breasts and ties behind her neck. The girl's eyes shine dark and smiling out from long lashes that glance often towards our table. Her brown hair cascades over her shoulders. Just over four years older than me, I think. I get a knot in my gut, and look at Dad. Dad and Bill watch the girl too. I watch Dad laugh to himself as he looks at the girl. I know that something is not right about his look, or his laugh, and a helpless feeling of entrapment creeps over me.

I clear my head. I sip the last of my soda. It is bubbly water with thick sugar at the bottom of the glass. Its grit makes its way up the straw and tastes so sweet on my tongue. Greta and I run behind a curtain and put on our swimsuits. We head to the pool while Dad and Bill finish their beers, then disappear somewhere. The pool does not have enough water to swim in, we discover when we get closer, but Greta and I make the best of it. We throw small flowers into the brackish water and sit on the edges of the huge, concrete bowl, and dangle our toes over the side.

The dark-haired girl takes off her high heels and sits down next to me. She looks at me and smiles. She puts her hand to her chest and says, "Natasha." "Becky," I say. Then she looks around with her big black eyes, and swings her long hair back over the blue sateen strap of her pantsuit and says, "Quinceañera!" and points to herself, putting up ten fingers, then closing one hand and then emphasizing five fingers. Fifteen. I know. Then I put up my ten fingers. I feel young. But old. I give her another piece of gum, wrapped in pink, and she stands to leave.

chapter seventeen

hymen

~~~~~~~~

The guide drives us back to the boat. The military guy with the square jaw is at the dock, and cannot hide his huge grin as Dad walks towards him. They grab forearms. We are handed a scroll-type paper, which says we are granted leave by the Cuban government. We pull anchor and set sail towards the Island of the Pines, then to the Cayman Islands. Just off Cuba is Dry Tortuga Island, an old fort, that we linger by. There are sharks swarming below us, nurse sharks on the white sand magnified through the clear water. A breezy few days' sail to Cayman.

April 29, 1982—Journal Entry

Today we woke up and we were heading for the Island of the Pines. We met a fishing boat and we asked them where the port was and they told us and when we got there the port wasn't where it was supposed to be so we have to sail straight through to the Cayman Islands. I am very mad that we did not get to go to port.

April 30, 1982—Journal Entry

Today we didn't do much but I did think a lot. I thought about Mom and my sisters. I also thought about school and my birthday (which is a long time away, November 22). Later on in the day a bird flew inside our boat and landed on my head. He flew in two more times and stayed in the boat half the night. He was so cute and tiny, he made a lot of noise too.

<hr />

We have run out of water and a wave broke into the boat onto my bunk, so all my clothes are wet and dank. There are red bumps on my skin, all over, that itch. When we dock, after sailing into the small port just off the main port of Grand Cayman Island, Dad's softness hardens as he steps onto the dock. I feel confused as the solid earth under my feet seems to heave, and I spin. Greta and Bill leave for the airport. After I help wash the decks and linens of salt water and help clean up our boat, I try to find fresh water and an open market for food, and Dad heads to the bar.

No sign of water. I find some snap peas and pineapple, chicken wrapped in rice. I see the bar where Dad must be, and a library across the street. I wander into the bar and immediately want to leave and go back to the boat, but see that I need to wait. Dad is eying a woman in the bar. She is blond and tan. Pretty in her plain naturalness. She sits at a table at the far end by the window and writes. Sometimes she looks up, as if in thought, her pen paused, then she catches Dad's stare. She smiles, looks down shyly, looks up again and meets his gaze deeply. I watch this from my corner table, from behind my book, the way he stares with his blue eyes. It makes me want to hide back in my book, in some other faraway story.

I see now that Dad is ready to leave the bar. He stands, his hand reaching to the table for balance. He plants his feet shoulder-width apart and bends his knees in a slight athletic stance. I know he will not make it back to the boat tonight, which means I won't. I see him wonder, as I do, if he can put one foot in front of the other. He is with a man who wants to take him somewhere, to look at land, or at a boat, to take him on some adventure.

The pretty blond appears and kisses his cheek, leaves her hand on his shoulder. She asks him something close to his ear, but he shakes his head. He looks at me and points, saying something to her. It must be about how I scratch my skin. She looks at me and comes towards me. My chest tightens.

"Hi, my name is Amelia," she says in a French accent. "Your dad said you might want to take a shower. My place is not so far." She smiles and regards me intently. I don't want to go, but . . . a shower. Probably fresh warm water and soap. And privacy. And rose oil to make me smell nice. I feel my skin layered with salt and dust and sun, red bumps. My hair is greasy at the roots, and impossibly wind-tangled. I can already feel sweet water over my eyelids, my shoulders, cleaning my feet. I look at Dad, his apologetic eyes, his nod. I look at her and nod, and stand to follow her out the door.

Her flat is small and clean and white. She shows me to the first floor only: a huge bed set on a carpeted floor, a wall closet with mirrored doors, and a white-tiled bathroom. She has asked a lot of questions about Dad. I answer in my standard way—briefly. Yes or no when possible. Mostly quiet. But now she asks about me. "Do you have your period?" I do not answer. She takes off her small blue sundress and sets it on the edge of her bed, now wearing only her nude thong bikini. "Put down your basket," she says, and pats the bed next to her. I step back and lean onto the bathroom door.

"Do you have your hymen still?" she asks. I do not respond. "Do you know what is hymen?" She looks at me and knows I will not break my silence. She shifts her gaze to the mirror and then loops her thumbs in the sides of her thong and inches it down, wiggling her bottom out of it until it is around her ankles. She flings them from her toes and they land on the carpet at the base of the closet mirror. "I don't have mine now." I see her reflection as she hikes her knees up, holding her shins with her small hands. I cannot help but stare in the mirror, at the folds like the opening of a shell, curving down then opening to a small black hollow. "It would be here." I startle as she slides her finger into the dark. I know it feels good, what she is doing. But she should not do this in front of me. "A thin layer of skin, like a drum, before you are penetrated."

I reach behind me and grope for the door handle and turn it. As it gives I fall back into the bathroom, close the door between me and her, and lock it, and slide to the cold white-tiled floor. Well, now I know about my hymen, I think as I look for a way to escape and to calm my beating heart. The window to the right of the shower is small but I can do it. The showerhead has a handle below it, that turns to both blue and red. Sweet warm water for my salt-encrusted skin. Can I risk that first?

chapter eighteen

cayman islands

Dad moves the boat a bit further away, to hide us from the woman. His girlfriend Emma is coming. I am excited for her singing, her flaming bunches of red hair falling over sparkling blue eyes. She is like a mermaid queen to me. We pick her up at the airport. She reviews all she has taught me: the capitals and countries of South America, and she sings to me in wistful, deep blues. Her visits to Colorado had turned to longer stays, to help Dad with me, but on Christmas morning when I saw that there was no one, nothing, around the bare tree in the stand downstairs, pine needles dropping on the tile beneath, I ran up to Dad's room to say good morning. Emma was trying to hide under the covers, but I could see the mounds of her breasts, and strings of her red hair straggling onto the pillow.

I revel in the new company. And I love living on the boat anchored in a bay, where I can go to the land whenever I desire. It is a blue, calm day. Dad has taken the dinghy ashore by the time the sun feels warm. Emma and I stay onboard, enjoying the calm, the coolness before the sun rises higher, the freedom without a man around. On the boat alone, we string shells on necklaces to wear on our tanned skin, and sew orange and turquoise patterned fabric to wear as wraps. She keeps pulling her tank top down then up, exposing her huge white boobs, and laughs and smiles. As we prepare to swim ashore, Emma somehow convinces me to swim naked, and it feels safe. "It feels so good! And there is no one around . . . this part of the island is isolated," she says.

We have a small dry sack in which we stuff our wraps, bathing suits, and flip-flops, some money, and my journal. I carry the sack with my arm raised above the water as we swim to shore. Diving in, I immediately feel the cool of the water caress my normally unexposed chest and bikini area. It is an exhilarating lightness, a liberation. We gasp in turn from the sensation as we emerge from the surface of the water. I reach forward in the saline buoyancy, with my one arm up, the other pushing the water away and to the side to propel me forward.

As we near the curve of the white beach, I feel a sudden panic. I see a quick flash from the corner of my eye, and remember the gold hoops in my ears, the thin necklace with the small, flat golden heart, hanging from my neck. The earrings and necklace Mom had given me for my birthday before she left, that I have never taken off. Barracuda, I know, are attracted to that glinting gold, not knowing the difference between its sparkle and that of a tiny fish. My heart pounds as I think of the sharp, pointed teeth. Such teeth had left big, brown, shiny stretches of scarred skin on the arms and ankles of children in Cuba and Dry Tortuga. I desperately propel myself forward, trying not to thrash and emit a smell of fear.

When I reach the sand, I slither, exhausted, up on my belly. Looking back to the bay, my breathing raspy, I see Emma splash water with her feet as she walks up the shore. I reach to my ear and remove one gold hoop, then the other, then undo the clasp behind my neck. I clutch the jewelry in my wet, dripping fist, realizing my nakedness. As soon as I reach the shore, I run up the beach to a stone wall where the sand meets the tropical foliage, trying to encroach upon the ever-drifting beach. Emma calls me to stay and swim, but sees my reluctance and follows up the beach. I place my gold jewelry on the top of the wall, and in doing so, peek over to see a cemetery choked in vines and purple blooms. I wonder who is buried there. We dry in the shadow of the wall, wrapping ourselves in the bright-coloured fabric; we don our shell necklaces and set off on a path towards the road. "Hurry up!" Emma calls, and I run down the path after her. In my haste and impatience for survival, I removed the only thing I had from my mom and forgot it there, on the warm cement wall in a small wet pile, calling the reflection of the bright yellow sun.

The path is overgrown with roots and large leaves, but it takes us to a small, primitively paved road. We walk on the chalky white gravel on the rough shoulder and hear crickets hum in the hot, moist air. After some time, we hear a rumbling and stop to wave at a truck coming from behind. The truck is small and rusted blue. It has a flat open bed on which a woman sits with a bale of something under her arm. She has a chicken and a boy by her other side. A young man stands on the bed with his rib cage pressed to the cracked glass of the rear windshield. He drums his palms on the roof of the cab. He turns his head and smiles at us with a long strand of grass in his teeth. The driver has a worn straw hat, and skin like smooth leather, and he slowly gestures to us, with the wave of an open palm, to hop on the bed of the truck.

I grab the outstretched hand of the boy and make my way to sit with my back to the cab, next to the woman with the chicken. Emma sits cross-legged facing me, holding on to one of my ankles for dear life, as the truck lurches forward, then slowly rambles on, followed by dust mingled with laughter and snippets of song.

In the town, I show Emma the open market. We marvel at the colours of the fruit, and the kind eyes of the women selling it. We slowly take in the shapes the green beans make next to the eggplant, and imagine the spices and butter I could sauté them in. Fresh, not canned food. The beauty of the goods spread on bright cloth envelops me and I begin to work my way to communicate with the women, about the freshness and the price. As if out of a dream, I hear the voice of Dad yell from somewhere. I had been hearing it, but it took some time for it to penetrate my present state of consciousness. "Ahoy there!" the booming voice sounds from across the street. Emma and I turn from where we stand in the market, and slowly walk to meet Dad.

Dad is gregarious and revved up. He has already returned to his booth, with new friends, as we enter. "He runs a rum distillery! Third generation. The guy who picked us up. He gave us a tour of the cane fields, the operation, and wants to take us diving . . . they let the rum age for years in barrels underwater!" Dad is beside himself telling his friends. He quiets, his eyes sparkle as he sips his rum. He watches the people, loving life, the fortune he stumbled into. Emma and I are equally enamoured, enchanted by the romance, the seduction of more.

The bar, the same bar, has wide-open windows that let the breeze of the ocean pass through. Dad has set up camp at his large wooden booth, in the front of the restaurant, with a view of the street, the wharf, and all passers-by. The booth is conveniently yelling distance to the bar where the drinks are poured. Dad and his friends have collected an arsenal of bottles, and their slurred words already are poised for combat. I order a 7UP and listen, trying to follow the nonsense the men make sound so important.

After some time at the bar, out the window from the booth I see that whitewashed building across the street again, with LIBRARY printed in golden letters over the arching door. Dad wants me to stay near, but I run back and forth to collect books to read, when the live entertainment becomes too much to bear.

Dad is slurring when I leave, the din in the bar weighing me down, and I feel groggy from the dim light that struggles to seep in through the smoke and thickness of adult talk, despite all the windows.

I slither under the booth and walk out the open door, nearly blinded by the sun. *Heart of Darkness* (Dad told me about this book and said I should read it), Judy Blume, Emily Dickinson poems, and Nancy Drew are on the list running through my head. A man at the bar makes me think of Marlow . . . this whole trip makes me think of Marlow in *Heart of Darkness*.

Though the arching doorway, the stacks of books framed majestically inside, I walk. I can smell the rich must of history in the dusted light, and my fingers graze reverently on the spines of many stories as I wander down the aisles.

I am looking down, reading the back of Nancy Drew's *Ransom of the Seven Ships*, as I walk catatonically out of the library, onto the bright, bustling street. A piercing noise deafens me, a blaring horn. I look up from the book, shameful of my carelessness, into the eyes of the driver. I feel the stillness in the street. People stop and stare.

Someone yells from the open window of the bar, "Watch your driving . . . Bloody hell!" I and the driver remain frozen, mid-street, as the others begin to resume movement. I feel dirty, hot, encrusted dust on my leg from the near-collision with the car.

I look back down to the back cover of my book and slowly resume my pace. I cross the street to the worn path in crabgrass, turn by the bougainvillea blooms, and go up three steps to the veranda of the bar. This is life on land. It does not feel safe, though there is some mysterious protection over me.

I spend too much time at that booth, even with Emma and Dad, listening to stories of different characters that take the stage. Some interesting, some mundane. Some just drunk.

chapter nineteen

jamaica

~~~~~~~~

All I remember of Jamaica is Emma. She is the anchor to reality. After we sail there and stay on the boat for a bit, we rent a white two-story apartment on Montego Bay. Friends of Dad told us about it. It is simple and clean, with beautiful fans. It has a small kitchen with a gas-fired stovetop, so I know that I can eat, and there is a little bed with clean sheets, so I know that I can sleep. Emma shows me the breadfruit tree out our door. I peel and fry the fruit and it tastes good, especially with butter and sugar.

The bar Dad chooses here is called Rick's Café. It must be famous. I like to be there, not only because Emma talks with me, plays cards with me, sings at the bar, introduces me to people, but because it sits high on cliffs, and people jump and dive, suspended in air for long moments, into the beautiful blue ocean below.

When a woman offers to braid my hair, Emma looks at my dad and he says yes. Emma sings with the other musicians, as she always does. There is a blond man with a moustache and guitar. He wears a New York Yankees jersey and his name is Michael O'Keefe. It turns out he is an actor and friends with James (Jim) Woods. Jim likes to go into the shore break with a woman in the evening, to hug and kiss her there.

I see what they do underwater when Emma and I snorkel out to Dad on the boat. I am so distracted I don't notice when it gets shallow and the tide suddenly goes down and there are thousands of sea urchins millimeters from our bellies. I can hear them snapping underwater. Their talk lets me know I am safe, though I still suck my belly in. On our way in Dad stands up and steps on a stingray. Its tail strikes right between his big and next toe. A clean but deep hole. "Pee on dat," the local lady insists. Jim saunters out of the water holding his lady's hand and laughs at Dad.

June 14, 1982—Journal Entry

Monday today. We ate breakfast of rice then a girl came by with a breadfruit and pineapple. Then Peter, a new friend from a neighbouring boat, came over and said he called home and they said that they got busted for cocaine and forty of his friends got busted too. The police are looking for him in Key West, Florida, but thank God he's here. Then we went to the post office and mailed letters. That same morning, I took my hair out of braids and my hair was kinky. I loved it. When we got back from the post office, we ate lunch with Peter then came back to the room and laid around. Then we went to bed. Emma and I stayed up to 12 talking and then Peter came at 12:30. He told us that immigration was on his boat and the boat next to theirs. The boat next to theirs said there is a secret agent on the *Oceanie* (Peter's boat), so Peter is really scared.

At Rick's Café Emma orders me sugar drinks and I am happy. Even though there is a home to go to that is secure, with bed and food, I still somehow end up on the adventures. There is a young man named Sie who catches Dad's interest. We go with him in a small car and drive up winding fruit-strewn roads to look at property. By now I know this is a game for Dad, and that there are probably drugs involved. The music we listen to is Bob Marley and Bob Dylan. The words soothe my soul with their magical emergence of story and passion. I think Dad follows the story line of "Isis." My whole life could be portrayed with Dylan's album *Desire*. He likes his friends to give him mystery, risk and adventure, and he likes to give that back. He gives that to me, whether I like it or not.

Sie brings out a huge mushroom and smiles. His black skin is satin and smooth, his teeth are white. He has dried portions of the mushroom in a baggie, along with some weed and some sticky brown resin. They eat them and smile as we drive. We stop often to say hello to women and children. A Rasta man so beautiful—young and muscled, smiling with love of a wife and baby by his side. He sits with his machete in a stalk of freshly cut plantains on the side of the road.

I climb banyan trees and pick mangos. I find sticky sap that lights on fire. I pet baby goats that suck on my finger and collect blue eggs from chickens. Another lady braids my hair and asks me questions about my life. Then the bugs come out and it is dark. I smell fire and hear the change of voices from Dad and Sie. I wish I had stayed home in bed, though I know it is worth it to see and feel and smell this land. Jamaica. Rasta. But now I pay the price. The night is long and I am tired and hungry.

On the way home a car follows us. After a time it puts a light on its roof that spins blue. Dad and Sie hand me the bags with dried mushrooms and weed and the brown paste and tell me to put it in my pants, in my underwear. I do. And I know to be quiet and play sleep when we stop. They won't hurt me. I am protected. We pull to the side. Our car is hot, the only sound the buzz of three flies. The man in the car behind opens his door, I see his brown pant legs rest for a while on the ground before he stands. My heart beats quickly. The man leans into Dad's window, and Dad smiles and asks about the land. His family. Tells him he must have a beautiful young wife. He invites him to Rick's Café for a drink, and we drive off.

Dad meets the man who pulls us over at Rick's the next day. Emma leads me to the bar and orders me a sugar soda and takes me to the cliffs to watch the divers as Dad leaves somewhere with the man.

chapter twenty

magic ocean watch

~~~~~~~~~~~~~~~~~

We sail from Jamaica to Marsh Harbour, Great Abaco, which I remember well from my first visit when I was about six. *Cattle Creek* will stay there for a bit, then Dad will sail through the Panama Canal into the Pacific Ocean. Emma has to leave but Amit will meet us in Marsh Harbour. Dad explains his plans to me as we motor out of the little harbor and enter the open sea.

The winds rise and Dad puts Brahms's "Requiem" into the cassette player and turns it up full volume. Violins sing to accompany a lull in the wind, flutes whistle in encouraging harmony to the vibration of the stay wires. Dad knows German and in a low voice, ascending in volume, with the whispering horns and strings, sings, "Blessed are they that mourn, for they shall be comforted," the opening lines of the mass. How appropriate, I think as my eyes scan the darkening sky. A flash of lightning spreads across the slate-blue, rolling ocean in the distance. My chest fills with a fullness of dread, then turns to comfort with the instrumentals vibrating in the depth of my heart, as the water sloshes against the hull of the boat.

I crawl from the cockpit, through the companionway down to my bunk. I secure the leeboard. It is six p.m.; I have four hours to sleep before my watch. We set it up that way—four hours on, four hours off. You can do whatever you want in the off time, pending attention to the boat first and foremost, but sleep is the most practical option. Falling asleep is either impossible, or, I hit the pillow like a dead weight. Sometimes, at two o'clock in the morning, I am wide awake staring at the lacquered wood above my bunk. My mind reels from the magnetism of the full moon, the plankton trailing behind us. Other times, I have to resort to plucking nose hairs to keep awake, and there is no question about what I will do in the "off" time.

Now, the music lulls me to sleep and continues on in my dream. A long, sinewy rope dangles from the clouds. It is made with a hand-twined natural fiber, which is dripping with silvery wet. It has barnacles and seaweed growing from it. The wind blows the bitter end to me, as I sit alone on the aft cockpit locker. I wear a harness when I am on watch alone, which is tied to the lifeline, in case a stray wave might try to wash me over, which is common enough. I watch, in my dream, as the wind blows the rope towards me, inviting me to grab on. It stretches from somewhere high in the billowing bulges of heavy grey clouds, and lists towards me, wantonly. I can see small faces of sea fairies clinging to the rope, with pursed red lips and glistening eyes. Their hair is a strange coppery red that drapes over the seaweed, small wisps releasing and blowing in the wind.

The wind is strong, and the waves come heavily from astern. The boat surfs down the faces, sometimes lurching from the crest. I am tired and know that if I just reach out to the small, inviting hands of the sea fairies, and grab onto the rope, I will be fine. I will drop for a time into the dark, cool water and swim with dolphins, and strange no-eyed creatures, and then I will be lifted, entwined in the rope, to the sky, to a heaven. My hand slowly reaches for the rope.

I wake suddenly as Dad softly shakes my shoulder. "Hey girl. It's your shift." He hands me the mug full of steaming brew, which we make for each other at the beginning of each shift. It is a mixture of powdered milk, Ovaltine, and instant coffee. It is syrupy, thickly sweet, but warm and soothing to a sea-nauseous belly. It is ten p.m. I peek out of the companionway to check the sky, and see that the clouds have lifted, giving way to a light emerging from the moon. The wind has calmed, as have the seas, but there still could be showers. I don my thick yellow rain pants and a long-underwear shirt, carrying up the rain slicker to have just in case.

As I scan the horizon, I listen to Dad's report: "The bearing's still 342 degrees true, give or take, and won't change for days. It's all just open ocean out there. We're not in any shipping lanes, but I did see the hind end of a cargo vessel at about 20 degrees a few hours ago. Just look out for those beasts, and any others that might sneak up on us. Wake me up if the wind comes up and you need to take in sail . . . or if anything else gets you going. I'm right down here, Bexter girl." I jump down the hatch quickly to log the time and heading on the chart, adjust the declination for the magnetic heading and the variation of the compass, which is only slight, and then reappear in the cockpit for my watch. I stand on the stern bench and look out at my amphitheatre.

I am a bit groggy, but awake. The first two hours go by quickly, as I get into a rhythm pulling and pushing the tiller just so, to surf perfectly down the larger swells. There are signs of dolphins at the bow, but it is too dark to see, and just too big a sea to let the tiller go. I see dark, silky flashes in the moonlight, and small sprays, but it could just be the sea splashing playfully against the bow. I imagine I hear dolphins call, squealing softly, but that could be the wind, or water too. By the end of the third hour I begin to get sleepy. The moon is full and out, and the swell becomes small enough to lash the tiller in place with line so the boat can steer herself.

I stand and look over the small cabin, with my hands resting on the wooden beam that Dad had constructed as a frame to act as a traveler for the mainsheet. It is the perfect height for a ballet bar, so I use it to practice pliés and relevés and try to keep my legs from cramping. I giggle at my animated attempts of grace on the ever-moving surface. When my muscles start to burn, I try to distract my mind, fill it with French conjugation, or do math multiples. Eventually the beauty of the moon lures me, and I have to sit, in my fatigue, pinching my checks to stay awake. Counting the minutes. No ships passing. Same heading.

She's carrying us along just fine, I think. Thank you girl, thank you God—whatever you are out there. I see the moon as a window to people I miss, or do not know but long to miss. They might be hiking up a mountain in Colorado, looking at the same moon. Can they see me? I wish I could see them. I wish they could be with me, or I with them. 13:49. Counting the seconds to sleep.

When I wake we are docking in front of the Conch Inn. Amit has smiles and bread for us, beer for Dad and ginger beer for me. Amit hates sailing. "Land Man," Dad calls him. Because Dad cannot wait to get to port where Amit can find anything he, or anyone else, wants, which is usually luxury and women. Both he and Dad use me, like a cute puppy, in the bars, to attract women. And I crave the attention. I also love the bars there: big, open palapas where all of us—kids, teens, my dad and Amit and the women they meet, and the grandmas and grandpas—play dominos, eat, talk, dance and live life. We always dance. Me the only white girl with all the other young black kids, who teach me the organized, choreographed dances they make up. I sing and dance and the nights are beautiful and I never want to sleep. After dancing I make Dad and Amit and the ladies jump into the glassy black water with me, under the stars.

Here I want to stay. But I cannot. We have to leave. Again. There is school. There is work.

chapter twenty-one

colorado

~~~~~~~~~~

It is almost time for me to be back in school. Mom and I are in Colorado at the cabin. She cranks the handle to grind raw meat in a metal grinder viced to the counter. I think this is strange, but she seems content. I will go to sixth grade this year. Mom takes me to the little mall in Glenwood and buys me a pair of pants and a pleated turquoise shirt. Mom and I usually hand-sew my clothes or buy them from thrift stores, so I want to wear these every day.

Dad has finished building onto the cabin, that design he kept talking about, that he sketched on the back of his Copenhagen can. It is like a windmill, an octagon base made with creosote-soaked, reused railroad ties. The smell permeates the living room. The living room is on the bottom and has a potbelly stove that we stoke with coal; it fills the room with smoke, which also adds to the smell. The windows are large and angle in as the building gets narrower as it goes up. There are open wooden stairs that go to the next circular floor, which is Mom and Dad's bedroom. Or was. I don't think he is coming back here anymore.

The bed is built in and I have to climb up to get on because it is so high. Above the bed is a wooden landing suspended by chains; I can reach up there from the bed and pull myself up, and then there is a ladder that goes to the smallest circle on top. Every floor has these huge windows that look out to the Colorado plateaus and the snow-dusted mountains. The oak is turning red and the aspen leaves on the distant hills are pinkish-orange.

At the very top, if you stand on the built-in desk, there is a hatch to a tiny little loft under the peak of the tower. When the wind blows it shakes and sways up there. Lightning is attracted to the top of the tower and when it strikes the whole structure trembles and cracks. Sometimes the phone rings from the lightning and the receiver jumps out of its cradle.

When Dad gets back to Colorado from sailing I am relieved. He is tanned and smiling. He takes me to his new construction site. He asks me to help him lay out the rooms of the house to make sure every room has the best view and most sun. There is a pile of redwood that I climb up. It is recycled from an old barn in northern Colorado. Dad will use it to frame the house. We sit on a stack of bricks as he rolls a joint and tells me how the home will be built.

There are tall pot plants growing in the disturbed soil around the construction site, from all the seeds Dad and the guys he's building with toss out of the weed they separate and roll up into thick joints. I smell the smoke, with the cooling sagebrush and the mustard weed that swarms with honeybees.

He takes me to the Black Nugget Saloon on his motorcycle. It is late and I am tired. I remember looking closely at the faded blue-linoleum floor. Trying to sleep, I see the metal base of the bar stool and notice how it is attached to the floor. There is black sticky grime collected there. I fall asleep with that vision, and the noise grinding in my head.

Dad is a handsome man. He has a lined face that hides the insecurity of his heart. Crystal-blue twinkling eyes, and a Cheshire cat grin. Muscular and of medium stature, and always fit. His eyes grow wild, unpredictable, when he drinks, and his smile becomes menacing. One leg is shorter than the other due to some accident, which causes him to walk as though he is always trying to catch his balance, which often he is. When I wake up that is how he walks. I am nervous about our motorcycle ride home, but hold on tight and let go. I see the stars blurring overhead.

This summer I feel that he teaches me to be independent. Confident. Tough. "Don't let them see your face until you get a feel of who they are," he says. I am starting to develop breasts, and he buys me an oversized, dark blue, Everlast brand sweatshirt with a huge hood that I can tuck all of my hair into, and hide my face in. The gait of my walk does not give me away yet, and I can climb, run, wrestle, just like all the boys.

He shows me how to pick up, unlock, load, and shoot the .22. We go for cans he sets up in the sagebrush and cactus. At first when my bullet hits, a cloud of dust plumes up and the can reappears unscathed. Then I jump the can five feet in the air. Then I hit a hole clear through the can and it stays put.

When this house is finished we can move into it and actually stay for a little while, he tells me. Somehow I know my mom won't stay here with us.

There are a few days left before school starts and I spend it at the community pool, loving the time with other kids. At the end of that summer, before my twelfth birthday, I get my period at the Carbondale community pool. I am standing on the side about to dive in and my friend points to the watery pink dripping down my leg. Dad picks me up later and I have to tell him so we can go to the Safeway and buy something to take care of it. Afterwards, we drive home in silence. Hot summer air smelling of sun-drenched sagebrush hits my face through the open window. The truck tires roll over the loose gravel in front of our house as we come to a stop below the wooden deck that looks out to Mount Sopris. Charlie comes out onto the deck to greet us.

Charlie stands in the same place I had been a few months earlier when I watched the small frame of my mom step out of her car in the drive, this time wearing a red Chinese-style dress, high heels trying to navigate gravel, blond hair in curls. When Dad greets her, she says, arms straight and shaking at her side, "Nikki? This time you slept with Nikki? My friend?" I see her tears glint in the sun as she looks up at me, her goodbye, before she disappears in her grey sedan behind a cloud of dust through which grasshoppers jump in an arc.

Now, Dad emerges from the truck, raising the box of Kotex pads up over his head for Charlie to see, and Charlie reaches his arms to the sky and pronounces one of his common prayers, or invocations, that come before a big life event. "Land beyond, beyond! She is a woman now!" I shrink in the cab of the truck. Charlie coaxes me out by offering me a chocolate ice cream bar and a beer.

I lumber up the wooden stairs and take the ice cream. I sit at the kitchen table with Dad and Charlie. Dad hands me a magazine with the weed shake, to sort out the seeds. Dad trims the buds. Charlie rolls.

"What is the land beyond, beyond?" I ask. "It is where and when there is freedom," Charlie says. "And God energy and spirit and the power of love. Endless possibilities, in balance," Dad adds. It is the mecca, the hajj, the magic guidance that I learn about, and struggle with, in the years to come.

chapter twenty-two

school

I start the public school this time as the leaves begin to fall. At school I get into fights because I am somehow different from the ranch and mining kids there. They say I talk funny, and I can't answer questions about why they haven't seen me around. Everyone has known each other there since birth. After a few weeks Dad begins to forget to pick me up from school. The bell rings like a fire alarm, lockers slam. Yelling, screaming, and laughing in the halls. Backpacks heavy with books, or not, slung over shoulders. I just watch, feeling like I am in an encased bubble walking slowly through it, looking out. I walk out alone, or maybe with my new friend Stacy, from the safety-glass front doors of the little red-brick middle school in Carbondale, and sit on the cement parking block in front of the bike rack.

I watch as the school busses pull in, the kids load up. Kids walk down into the little town to their cozy little wooden houses, with smoke curling out of their chimneys.

Moms and dads open car doors and squat to hug embarrassed little bodies that are shuffled into those cars. The bikes in the bike rack become less tangled, as they waver off with the ever-faster pedaling of kids with jeans bunched up over ankles. "Come over if you need to," Stacy calls over her shoulder as she finally leaves me to walk home. But I know Stacy's mom doesn't really like that.

Now I am the only one left in the parking lot. This is when I know I am real. My heart feels big and too heavy, and something in my throat swells up. Options run through my mind and cause me to worry. What if something happened to him? He must just be busy. If I walk to the bar and he is not there, I might miss him trying to find me here. But I know he is at the bar. Either there or at Moses Guerrero's house. Dad loves to box with him.

Moses is the only guy from Mexico in town. He has a big, wide, tan face, with a big, wide nose spread out right across it. It is a bit crooked and there is a scar reaching up from his chin, through his cheek, to the side of that nose. I only ever see him perched, like a big bear, on the bar stool—or "sparring," as they call it, with Dad. Dad gets that wild look in his eyes, and his sweat has a sweet, sour smell, kind of like beer, that flings off the soaked pieces of hair plastered to his forehead when Moses hits him on the chin.

The wind begins to swirl the dead leaves in the parking lot, and I know I have been there too long, so I stand up and walk. Just to the bar—three blocks from the schoolyard. Three blocks lined with perfect little Craftsman homes painted in pastel greens and blues. The bar—that is usually the best place to start. When I find him there, for a second I might smile, but then I just want to scream and hit him on the back.

On the bar stool, with his huge smile, at the end of the smoky room he sees me and yells too loud, "Come here!"

and swoops me up into a big, wobbly hug. Sometimes he even has a bit of drool on the corner of his lip. "Look at her," he shouts to someone hunched on the bar stool next to him. "Look at her! She is beautiful. . . ." The 'I' lasts awhile. "And she is a damn good athlete. Strong like bull." Again the long 'l.' His hand gropes towards his mug on the bar, taking a few times to grasp the handle.

"Can we go home now?" I ask. I am hungry. He just smiles strangely and says, "When I am done." I point with my finger to the level marking the amount of beer left in his glass, searching to look him in the eye. Then I slink over to the Pac-Man table and pull out my homework. After a while my head starts to throb. The noise in the bar is the epitome of "din." In my head it is a long, slow drone, like when the sound speed on records is slowed down and lowers a few decibels.

Dad's beer is full again, then empty, and I plead for him to take me home. I don't think I cry. But my head has that sound, like the noise of a tank with those metal tracks grinding on the ground, slapping down on pavement, in a low, mechanical groan. My throat is tight again, and my stomach a bit sick, maybe with hunger, or maybe just sick. I need to leave.

chapter twenty-three

dr. manship

The headaches start again. A sensation of waves and a feeling of being underwater. And the loud noise, a deep hum and vibration, as if a snowplow is moving over me. And deep, slow pain. It happens in the locker room at school. I collapse on the cement floor by the bench. It happens after Ms. Cray, our middle school gym teacher, tells Carlie Ansel she has to change in the locker room, in front of everyone else, and we see that her underwear is made of rags sewn together.

It often happens in bars. The noise of people talking becomes a blur and trying to follow conversations is frustrating. Conversations where each person has a passion, or a sadness or joy or some adventurous story to share, but there is no connection. No back and forth of relatable information.

But we are leaving again. After school ends we drive to Utah then to California. This time we are not on the motorcycle but in a car with Dad's new girlfriend,

Deborah. And her son. Deborah goes back and forth between Aspen and LA and has pink nails, thick blond hair, and bright blue eyes. Her son is maybe seventeen and is hunched over, his bangs dangling in his eyes, his Walkman and earphones on. I smell the dry hot air and watch the familiar landscapes as we drive. Now we pass the old gas station in the middle of nowhere between Green River and Price. There is a huge glass cage with a boa constrictor lazing inside. But we don't stop this time.

The tension in the car is high because Deborah would prefer to fly. It is quiet. I like the quiet. I like to see the red and green crenulations of sandstone mesas and buttes, and smell the sage and the earth and the hot asphalt.

In Utah we meet Dad's wrestling friend, Ben, from college. His wife is making homemade tortillas. He owns a rafting company with his son, J.R., and they plan to take us down the Green River. He is telling Dad about a man who can heal my headaches. "Remember how that guy in football practice used to bang his head against the wall to numb his migraines? How he leaned, palms flat against the bricks, and just repeatedly leaned back, slammed forward, leaned back, slammed forward. This guy, Dr. Manship, he apparently healed him somehow."

Dr. Manship's home is small and off-white, in a 1960s-style subdivision outside Salt Lake City somewhere. We gather in his kitchen and after some talk with Dad, Dr. Manship takes me into a room and I lie down on a doctor's table. Wooden-paneled walls. Everything in the room looks brown. He asks if I have had any head injuries. I tell him about the kid who I was "going with" in school who punched me in the nose and broke it. How the teacher had left and we were all dancing on the table. He got pushed off, maybe by me, and came flying up in a rage and socked me. Apparently, we were on the rocks.

"This probably pushed your nasal bone back into your endocrine gland," he said. "I am going to try to move some bones in your head." So, he presses his thumb hard into the bone under my eyebrow and then sticks his other thumb in my mouth and finds the roof. He presses hard and tells me to hold still and the pressure is unbearable. But I feel the shift. He removes his thumbs and takes my hands and brings them to my pelvis. "Press your fingers on the top of your pubic bone, as often as you can. At least five times a day." It all feels strange and on the verge of something I should run from. But I know Dad is in the next room. And I want the headaches to go away.

We go back to the kitchen table and Dr. Manship tells Dad, "We shifted some things and I have given her some exercises. And no sugar, caffeine, or processed white food for three months, then limit it." Dad and I say goodbye and thank you. As we walk to the car, I wonder if what the doctor has prescribed will work.

The car ride is full of questions that I don't want to answer. It seems like forever before we get to the river. I am relieved to meet Ben and J.R. at the launch site, where we help unload coolers and dry bags from the white van into the rafts. The river is glassy calm and the water skippers indent the surface with their tiny feet. It smells like cottonwood and the silt of Utah rivers in summer.

Ben has another friend, Brent, who has a daughter, Maxine, who is also fourteen. J.R. works with Ben as a river guide. J.R. is tall and dark and I like his shoulders, and the indented curve at his hips that disappears into his shorts. While we load, Deborah sits in the car, her outstretched fingers on the steering wheel, where she touches up her pink nail polish.

The first part of the river is hours of calm. My brain has curiosity burning, and I struggle feeling like I am not able to talk. I expect others to be telepathic. There is so much time to think. So much to see. Flying over the Mother-hole Rapid, Big and Little Joe. Deborah disappears from the boat on Little Joe. She emerges from the water on the other side looking drenched and miserable. She stays that way for the rest of the trip. We sleep outside and stay up late looking at the stars. The ground is covered with crickets. On Friday the thirteenth the rivers funnel us into Warm Springs Rapids, with huge rises and then drops of rushing, churning, paddling, spraying. I smile and grip the entire ride.

We spend time on the riverbanks studying, J.R., his buddy Brent, Maxine, and I. I don't remember Deborah's son on the trip. I think he was unhappy with his mom. But J.R, Brent, Maxine and I always study, drink, and tell stories. We hold hands and enter Whispering Cave. It is black and cold and damp. The wind really whispers inside. J.R.'s hand is warm and holds mine tight. I drink, maybe too much, and discover all of the constellations. J.R. tells me about Mecca, a land beyond, the paradise. Maybe shows me some of Mecca too. "I would ask you to marry me if you were older," he tells me. "I have never met anyone like you and things are so easy and fun with you." He tells me this. I know he has a girlfriend.

He drives me, after more rapids and stars, to meet his mom. And then he takes me to the Hilton to meet Dad and Deborah and her son at the hotel. "Hey beautiful, save yourself for me. I will write to you when you get to school." And he did, write to me at least. And, I didn't have a headache the whole trip.

chapter twenty-four

saat kaur

July 3, 1986—Journal Entry
Deborah, her son, Dad, and I drive towards LA, through
Reno. Through Las Vegas. I have not had a headache in a
few days. Dad says I talk and look different now. "You're
a motormouth, you look happy," he says. J.R. is on my
mind. I have never felt this way before. My heart feels
gelatinous and pulsating, raw and exposed. I am happy,
though so miserable.

On the drive we listen to the recordings Deborah has
of her Sikh. I learn that a Sikh is anyone who believes in
one immortal being, and follows tradition like wrapping
their head in a distar, and waking early and meditating
to cleanse from all sins and negativity.

We meet Deborah's daughters. They are models and
I look at the photo shoot they just did. I feel small and
ugly and insignificant around them. They are so pretty.
That night I get a headache and need to sleep.

I meet Deborah's, and now our, Sikh. Saat Kaur. A small woman wearing white, head wrapped. We talk a lot. My dad makes me meet with her again. "You think you are understanding of your wants and needs and desires," she tells me. "You figure that you do not matter. It is like you are married to your dad, have so many responsibilities for your age. You must stop holding things in."

We visit Malibu, a beach club, and stay in a nice hotel. I have never seen anything like this before. We have lunch next to Madonna and Sean Penn. We see the movie *Top Gun* and it reminds me of J.R. I am going to boarding school. I have to take entrance exams, the SATs, and they are hard but I do well. It sets in that Dad is sending me away and I am upset.

We leave Deborah and her kids, and LA, and drive north. Deborah is upset with Dad for all his smoking. He is depressed as we drive to San Francisco. We meet Amit and Charlie, and Emma, who Dad is still friends with. Dad drinks a lot when we get there. They all want to take me to my new school.

Dad has been depressed a lot lately. It is his birthday and I spend the afternoon cooking. I read his journal and it leaves me in tears. I fear him a little now because, well, I don't know why. I am just seeing a different side of him that was hidden before. He writes that he cannot trust women. He says he loves Deborah but calls her a fucking cunt. He says he has so much grief and wrath against his mother. That she was sick and ruined his life.

Lately I feel so much confusion, but it does not bring me so far down like it sometimes can. I feel so adult in my responsibilities, and in the mirror I see a reflection of a mature, slightly unhappy woman—not a fourteen-year-old girl. There is something in my face that seems strange to me. I am confused about who I am and how I am supposed to act, and what it even is to act like myself. My childhood is slipping fast, soon to be locked up into a chest that will fill and fill until one day it bursts open.

Dad takes me on the back of Amit's motorcycle to school—an all-girls Catholic boarding high school, chosen at the suggestion of Deborah. Amit, Emma, and Charlie ride in Charlie's RV. We drive to Santa Catalina School in Monterey, California, and park in the lot in front of the Virgin Wall, which shields the Catholic church. Ms. Sally and Sister Laura come out, alarmed at the sight of us. They won't let Dad behind the wall. He hugs me and sends me off with my duffel bag. I walk the path with Ms. Sally and her very long hair, and Sister Laura. I can tell she is spunky in her motherly, strict way, behind those glasses, in her blue habit. The other moms rush in with new bedcover sets from Macy's and Clinique face-washing sets. I realize people here have money. I did not know we had money.

The work here is impossible. I have not had all of the academic training that these girls have had, and I am pissed. I am determined to raise my grades. Having money is not what counts, so I will shine with what does. But the money part is hard. I feel out of place. At least we wear uniforms, so I don't have to wear my hand-sewn, hand-patched "migrant worker outfits," as Dad calls them. When I called him the other day, he did not seem happy to hear from me. I woke him up.

chapter twenty-five

sextant

<center>~~~~~~~~~</center>

On one of the school breaks I meet Dad and the boat in Port Allen, Kauai. He puts me to work and tells me, "You work for something you want. You learn from the bottom up. And if someone wants to hire you after you show them how much you want it, you get it." I clean the lockers from his passage from the Panama Canal. He for some reason thought the chocolate diet drink, Slim-Fast, would sustain him, so there are maybe fifty cans in the lockers below the bunks. That is where the smell comes from. Some cans are open and empty, some have exploded and seep chocolate ooze to slosh with the condensation, the bilgewater, and the cockroaches and mice that love it, until it drowns them. I slosh it out with my bare hands, gagging. Then mop it with rags. Then wipe it with water. Again and again until it is clean.

He takes me on sails around the island to teach me how to navigate. Dad does not navigate with modern instruments. When he wants to use the sextant, I become quiet. "Take the tiller," he tells me. He jumps below to get the wooden box with the sextant, opens it and brings it above decks to take a sun sight from the horizon.

He swears, and I want to help him. He tries to hold the metal eyeglass stable and dial the knob to obtain a correct reading of our location. I sit next to him to write down the numbers he calls. They are the angles of the sun to the centre of the Earth relative to our location. This is sine and cosine. The math in school offers no relevance. Here it is everything. It is survival. And I am overwhelmed. He hands the sextant to me, to learn. He wants to teach me. My hands are trembling and cold.

I hold the black metal and try to find a stable horizon. To mark down the correct numbers is crucial. Is this the angle? I am supposed to find the arc to determine where we are to sail, and compensate for magnetic deviation, for current and wind speed. Find the latitude by the sun? And he is now below. I know I cannot ask him. I brace myself with the sextant on my lap and look through the sun and star charts again. Tears burning in my eyes. My throat tightens. I cannot do it the way Dad wants.

No one can, I realize years later. But somehow, I love being here and going through this. I love the sea like I love oysters. The salt and texture. Horseradish and lemon. The sand and the grit. And the risk. Sometimes you might get a bad one. Dad seems introspective and quiet. I have a new perspective, maybe from some time away from Dad. I now notice these things on the boat, and about Dad, that never caught my eye before.

And though the sea is my home and *Cattle Creek* my sister, Dad now has someone aboard who is aware and who is asking questions. Who wants to know why things are done the way they are. That is his edge. He does not have the patience for these questions.

chapter twenty-six

molokai

～～～～～

June 14, 1987—Journal Entry

Graham is on board—Dad's spiritual friend who does
not drink. Graham is someone Dad met smoke jumping,
a practice for firefighting, in Utah. He is always fixing
things and figuring out how things work. He rigged up a
line from the front of the bowsprit to the forward bow of
the boat so he had someplace to hang on and swim underwater with the dolphins. I notice the book he brought on
board: Ouspensky's *In Search of the Miraculous*. His book,
a small duffel bag of belongings, the flip-flops, and the
clothes on his back are all he has. He and Dad talk about
God and nature. We are all profoundly silent when a grey
cloud, laden with moisture, pauses nearby. Or when the
moon lifts from the ocean like a heavy balloon.

Graham rigs up the dolphin line from the bowsprit
into the deep of the ocean between Kauai and Maui, Maui
and Lanai, Lanai and Moloka'i. He teaches me to lower
myself down onto it as we sail, letting the waves envelop

me while twining my legs into the line so I don't drift away forever. And flow, with the dolphins. Their eyes looking at me, my face pulled back smooth like theirs from the pressure of the sea, my hair flowing back. I hear them, their squeaking echo, and feel the vibrations of their noses waving through the cool blue sea.

In Maui we sit under the banyan tree and watch the fishing boats unload at the dock. Silver-bellied tuna. Octopus. Mahi mahi. I read in the grass in my sarong, *The Island of the Blue Dolphins*. I feel like I am reading a pure, more innocent version of myself. If only it were that simple. I want to be stranded on an island. Or even in prison . . . if only I have books. I know we will sail to Lanai soon and I feel like Karana.

The waves are choppy, steep, and blue, indicating the depth of the sea. Then the sharp contrast to sudden light ocean floor as the volcano reaches up towards us from below our keel. We anchor in Hulopoe Bay to a barren land covered with the spiky shrubs of pineapples, bulbs of golden fruit bobbing too heavily on top. Then the white sprawl of abandoned marbled terraces and stairs, lanais and columns, of the old Hotel Lanai.

We row the dinghy ashore and I feel like a spirit slinking to another time. A time of music drifting and long white ball gowns. Suits and white-brimmed hats. When the locals had no idea what was enveloping them. The stairs are long and cold and out of place in the warm tropic breeze. The palm trees sway and call us back to the boat.

Moloka'i channel rushes with heavy churning current and it takes us hours even though the island seems to be in spitting distance. We anchor off the old leper colony. I remember seeing somewhere when I was so young, maybe Borneo, maybe Greece, a man without half his nose, the hole so big and cartilage so sharp. "It eats your skin, leprosy," Dad told me then.

I read the book *Molokai*, by Bushnell. It describes the leper colony of the 1960s on the island, and the struggle for humanity while exiled there. Here Graham dives for lobsters. We feast on board. We don't go ashore.

chapter twenty-seven

kauai

~~~~~

In Kauai, we spend time with a family Dad had met earlier whose catamaran, *Tevaké*, is now in the same port as *Cattle Creek*. They have stopped in Kauai to work and take a break from the ocean. They have a son my age, Lucas, and a daughter a bit older. The mom is from New Zealand and is an artist. The dad is from England and has been on the ocean since the age of fourteen. They become family, our ocean family. We spend most of our time with these live-aboards who have sailed all around the world, recently taking a voyage from Hawaii to San Francisco, and then north up the coast to Alaska. They tell us about the twenty-foot tide surges in Alaska that lifted *Tevaké* into magical bays, jeweled with glaciers, then forced them to exit to the deeper Gulf of Alaska. I am in awe of them, this kind family. They take pictures and write about everywhere they go.

I imagine Lucas, working on the boat, on lookout with his spyglass, catching the swarms of sea life the Alaskan waters have to offer. Lucas and his dad were not getting along on the small confines of their boat, so after their trip to Alaska, Dad had invited Lucas to live with him in Colorado. Dad had already sent me away to that boarding school in California, to which I now return.

I am lonely back at school. The nuns and uniforms, the Virgin Wall, feel oppressive. At first, I shrink in the confines so opposite the freedom that is too big for me with Dad. He lets me come back to Kauai when school is out for summer to help work on the boat.

That next summer in Kauai, I get to know Lucas better. He and his dad are repairing *Tevaké*. They are still in the same industrial dock, Port Allen, in Kauai, where Dad is preparing, or recovering, *Cattle Creek* for or from some big journey. Not many sailors have kids, at least in the places we end up. So Lucas and I have an immediate curiosity for one another.

Lucas and I do a lot of the same work on the boat—the yucky cleaning, polishing, painting, sanding, organizing— but his dad works him harder. When Dad gets frustrated, dripping in sweat in the heat and swearing under his breath, he sends me to the marine shop for some caulk or tape or something. But Lucas's dad tells him to get his ass over here and work harder. Sometimes I catch Lucas's eye in those moments, so we can sneak away behind the rock jetty together, before the brewing anger escalates, and pretend we are busy with something important. We are accomplices in our escape, throwing rocks at crabs on the jetty, or starting fires in tin cans, or just sitting to look at the ocean or the other boats. I often notice Lucas just staring into the horizon over the ocean, or at the clouds. I ask him what he sees, and he says he just feels lonely. I understand.

part II

chapter twenty-eight

young adulthood

~~~~~~~~~~~~~~~~~~~~

Dad takes several years off from sailing, and I continue my high school, the all-girls Catholic boarding
school. I smoke weed, because I know how to roll a joint,
or make a pipe out of anything, and I drink, because I
think it is grown-up. When my friends and I get in trouble
and some of them get kicked out, I realize I am taking for
granted my situation. So I study. I get As. I stay on honor
roll and take as many AP classes as I can. I am so grateful
this school has so much to offer me and I try so hard. I
feel inadequate and unprepared, but I am in awe of what
they provide for me. For money, I work in the kitchen.

With Lucas's help, Dad builds houses and begins work
on a new subdivision in Colorado. Dad meets women, as
he does, and has adventurous, tumultuous affairs, one
resulting in a brief marriage, which ends as roughly as
it does quickly. The ocean begins calling him again, and
he formulates a plan for a journey through the Pacific
Islands, starting in Vanuatu. He will leave after doing

some work on *Cattle Creek*, which is still in Kauai. Dad tidies up his affairs, and makes his way to Hawaii with Lucas. There, he and Lucas reunite with Lucas's family, who had settled there semi-permanently a year before. He invites Lucas to be his mate to sail to Vanuatu, where an old friend, Gregg, lives with his boat, the *Vulcan*.

I graduate from high school in 1990, at eighteen years of age. I continue my summer jobs working in Oregon at the ski camps on Mount Hood and at restaurants, then start my first year of college in Colorado. I work hard, but feel lost, sort of in between worlds. Wanting to sail and travel, but also to find my career, save money, and finish school. I stay a year and a half but halfway through my sophomore year, when I try to register for my classes, I am unable to. Until now, I had been fortunate enough to have Dad pay most of my tuition. But now, I have no idea where Dad is, so I bounce around and work as much as I can.

Dad tracks me down and invites me to fly to Port Vila, Vanuatu, as soon as possible, to meet him and Lucas after they sail there. I am elated. Dad had not wanted me to be on the boat, much less even around, in my "teenage state of mind," for the past several years, and at twenty-one years of age I yearn for adventure, I am lost in this structured, normal life. The travel agent initially cannot even find Port Vila, but eventually, I am on an airplane, going to a mysterious place, to see Dad and little *Cattle Creek*.

May 15, 1993—Journal Entry

The plane is finally moving. I am tired. After Catalina, and college, I have plans. I will try staying near Mom and sisters, their home, on the East Coast so that I can get a career started. After this sail, in the fall I will finish my English exams. I will study art history and work in or write for a gallery. I will take extra classes at Temple and intern at the Philadelphia Museum of Art. I have worked so hard in school and am so excited to start working at something real—so I can travel for a living.

After ten hours we arrive in Fiji and Michelle Pfeiffer is on the same layover. She is pregnant and beautiful and carrying a dark-skinned baby. We smile. She is theatrical. I am behind her in customs. I am reading *Invisible Man*.

chapter twenty-nine

port vila, vanuatu

When I land, I make it through customs easily, and then go out to stand on the curb in front of the concrete airport building. Several taxi drivers laze against their cars. Ladies wrapped in colourful sarongs walk slowly with kids and baskets of goods in tow. I feel my throat and gut tighten, and a pounding in my head, recalling waiting hopelessly at school for the ride that never came. The air is warm, and the humidity feels thick on my skin. The smell of the sea and tropical flowers envelops me. I take a deep breath, clear my head, and then a man flags me down. "Becky! I am Rick," he says. "Hop in and we will get you to the harbour." We follow a pickup truck to the boat harbour, the back filled with a quiet, smiling mother of two kids in white uniform shirts. The schoolkids sing the entire way.

I can tell we are nearing a harbour by the change in the air. There is a light, refreshing breeze, and a deeper smell of the ocean. From the road, I can see the tops of boat masts bobbing just over the hill. Rick lets me out on the hot blacktop behind a palapa-style bar, beyond which is a concrete dock that curves out and becomes a pier. Rick waves goodbye, and so do the schoolkids in the truck in front of us, without a break in the smiles or song. I feel my own stillness as they continue on in motion.

The mast of *Cattle Creek* sways at the end of the dock. It is comforting to see her, floating gracefully on the water. Then I see Dad and Lucas, in the distance, tan and quiet, milling around piles of metal parts. I walk slowly down the dock, feeling apprehensive. Four years have passed since I have seen Lucas. His body has grown and become defined by all his work on boats. His hands taste of the sea, salty and like seaweed. I will know this soon.

Lucas finally notices me. "Bexter!" He drops a pile of wet line and comes to give me a hug. Something swirls inside me. Dad continues to fiddle with the metal fastener he is holding, which appears to be welded shut with corrosion. "Hey girl," Dad says without looking up. Then he throws the metal piece on the ground, walks over and puts his hand on my head and rustles my hair. "Ready for some work?" He points to the yellowed sheets piled on the dock. "Those need some help. So do the bunk coverings down below. How was the flight?" "Fine. Thanks for asking," I reply.

I drop my bag, and begin preparing the laundry in a bucket with the hose and some soap from the boat. Lucas and I eagerly catch up on all that has happened to each of us in the last few years. I am glad to see him. And, the family of this boatyard, Gregg and Josie and more, come to visit and welcome me while we work.

May 23, 1993—Journal Entry
Gregg and his girlfriend Josie are spunky and full of life. Rick, who picked me up from the airport, owns the bar,

which they call the office, and later he invites us out on a sail on his yacht *Big Smile*. The water is turquoise. The ocean breeze on my face and the sound of Big Smile cutting through the sea puts me in a trance. This is home, I think, as we dock below the Kava Lounge. We walk from the dock up steep stone steps lined with bromeliads and elephant ears. The sun sets and the light of the lanterns guides us to a deck under a thatched roof, with wooden tables and red embroidered pillows. Kava is popular here; it is a fermented root that is chewed and spit and mellows you out. It feels like mucus in my throat. Dad and Lucas and I cannot go to the bar with everyone else after we drink the kava. We feel light-headed, off-balance, and nauseous. Instead, we walk home and sleep on the boat.

On the weekend we go to Rick's farm and have sashimi and a pig roast. There is always swimming in the ocean, and intermittent rain. Lucas and I play pool and drink beer at the "office." On our way home the bushes beside the dock are rustling. The woman docked next to us has fallen into them because she was drunk. She is too wobbly to cross the plank to her boat, so we put her in the dinghy and hoist her onboard like a dead weight. Once onboard, her three Australian crewmates offer us rum and Coke. Before sunrise Lucas and I stumble to the beach and snuggle in under a catamaran pulled ashore. He kisses me. A nice kiss. It stirs something new in me for him.

Several more days of work, and each night we spend our time in the palapa bar. We visit Gregg's boat, *Vulcan*, which is moored in the turquoise bay out front. The locals, when not in church or school, crowd to watch us work on the dock, but they never come close to the bar. The bar seems to have the same group in it day in, day out. I quickly grow tired with the drunk men, the obscene, unrated, Rolling Stones videos that are always on, and the distance it creates between the lovely town and some of its people. I often read or walk, visiting people in the markets.

One night we are all called by Dad to plan for the voyage ahead. Rounds of Tusker beer keep coming, and they all keep drinking. Dad and the captain of a ship moored here are talking, and the captain apparently has some secret charts for the area that he wants to share with Dad. "Dinghy Girl!" Dad yells to me across the boat. I know that is my cue to start pumping the dinghy up and get it out in the water. Lucas and the Australian woman we had met are kind enough to help. The three of us stumble out laughing as we balance the wooden plank set up as a bridge from the dock to the boat, to ready the dinghy.

We all pile in the small dinghy, nearly capsizing it as Dad and his captain friend stumble in. Lucas rows us out to the ship. It is massive and out of a fairy tale, like an old pirate ship. We climb up the rope ladder and over the deck rail, to a sprawling wooden deck furnished with a huge, wooden ship wheel. Dad and his captain disappear down below for some time, while Lucas, our friend, and I explore above decks. The stars sear through the pinholes of the velvet black sky, swirling slightly. Lucas's hand touches the small of my back, lingering there, as we look up at the constellations. My heart speeds and my cheeks grow flush.

We swing through the stays, climb the masts, and run over the decks of the huge ship, before Dad and the captain finally emerge. We row home, pouring back onto *Cattle Creek*, and all but pass out in our bunks when we hear Dad yell, through the giggles of the woman, "The charts! We left them!" Lucas's face is already smashed against his pillow, eyes glued shut. I crawl up the companionway ladder to the cockpit, over the rail into the dinghy and row back to the ship.

The night is still and the stars are still piercing bright in the black sky. The water is glassy ebony and makes gentle lapping sounds against the dinghy as I pull on the oars. I marvel at my adventure, wondering what I am feeling for Lucas, and what my future holds. I climb up the side of the ship quietly, see the charts on the benches where we had left them, and stealthily return them to *Cattle Creek*.

May 26, 1993—Journal Entry

The evening is bright and beautiful. That time when everything is almost silhouette and the sunken sun still reflects on the water. I just took a shower and am content. Lucas and I explored today. We drove around the island after cleaning the boat. We met a man who told us about an outrigger canoe that he made in two days. Lucas can talk to anyone. In the morning we do a shakedown sail to see how our little *Cattle Creek* is doing. I immediately feel how she and I sail together, how she whispers to me. Gregg patiently teaches me how to do little things to make sailing easier that Dad would never think to do.

chapter thirty

sail from port vila

The sail from Port Vila is good, with two days of wind and current following with us, so the boat is not too rough. We leave at three p.m. with Gregg, his girlfriend, Rick, our neighbour and her Australian crew, some of the village people, and of course everyone in the bar to see us off. I do not feel too sick but end up puking twice on my night shift.

As we set sail from Port Vila for good, Dad and Lucas start to drink and carry on. I don't remember Dad drinking so much at sea, and I am in sort of a pissy mood, having to check their navigation routes and headings on their shifts.

But as night sets I watch the plankton trail alongside us and everything is alright. I feel so comfortable on this boat. Lucas and I do our shift together, which I like. The worst part of the night is having to go down to go to the bathroom in the tiny, smelly head, because I am too shy to go overboard like I used to. It is so stuffy down below it immediately makes me nauseous.

We stop, for a brief stint, on one of the Maskelyne Islands about noon the next day. I look at the island, unable to speak. White sand, palm trees, clear water. We swim to land and explore and gather coconuts. It takes about an hour to circumnavigate the island. Mangroves crowd the leeward side. We collect fish. We spear a lobster. Eventually we start a fire and eat and drink beer and coconut milk. Lucas and I sleep half the night on the sand, where he kisses me gently, and his hands move over, then under, my sarong.

He seems far away and I like that. I guess he has his own trip going and he is immersed in his mind, which gives him a sort of depth and distance. Independence. I can't find that in many people.

That morning I wake up before the sun to voices and laughter. There are people fishing from their canoes, lingering at a curious distance. When they see that we are awake, they become more bold to approach. So beautiful and peaceful. They come just to talk and to offer us gifts of coconuts and mandarins. That concept seems like such a novelty compared to US custom. Several canoes surround *Cattle Creek* throughout the day, bringing more crab, pineapple, bananas, papaya, and squash. We give them Vatu, the local currency, and trade them this hideous canned curried chicken that Dad and Lucas think they will love. Terrible.

Dad and Lucas continue to gift cigarettes, bread, and more rum as the heat of yellow and orange melt into the water, and as the blue turns to ebony. A boy who sits next to me on deck has a shark-bite scar—mouth-shaped teeth marks on either side of his elbow. I point to his arm, wanting to gesture a story from him. He only smiles, looking to the things I have to trade: T-shirts, knives, coloured pencils, chocolate, drawings, and the hope of correspondence when we leave. We receive seared fish and squid cooked in a fire on the beach. The men in the canoes cough with each inhale of their cigarettes, trying to imitate Dad and Lucas's deep, long drags. I am lost to the men as the night goes on, and on my own I relish the fresh fish, not canned, as their hot juices drip down to my elbows.

In the morning, some boys bring Lucas and me out on their canoes to dive near a reef. We jump in to swim with kaleidoscopic fish, a turtle, a tiger shark. I love the colours. I am not even afraid of the shark, this time. We get back to the beach and all these boys and Lucas and I explore and laugh, and they help me find shells for my necklace. My magic necklace. They ask about America and the big cities there and if people kill each other. Sad. They ask Dad about God, which impresses him. They are all very religious. Beautiful people. Magical.

Standing on the deck, Dad sings an operatic tune as he moves to the foredeck to dump buckets of water over his salty, sweaty skin. His blue eyes glint from his weathered face as he raises his hand towards the sky with an exceptionally powerful vocal expression. There is a new silver streak appearing in his soft brown hair. Dad notices we are all quiet, waves, and stops his operatic bellows. "Bexter, Lucas, where's dinner?" His yell lifts the trance he has on me, and the other open-mouthed, wide-eyed onlookers, still circling us in their canoes. I close my similarly gaping mouth and narrow my eyes and get to making dinner.

~~~~~~~~~~

At dawn I hear a quiet rustle. The deep rich smell of coffee awakens me, and I peek out to see Lucas's flash of a smile subtly inviting me on an adventure. He hands me a cup of coffee, my sweatshirt and a sarong, and a machete. He has already loaded the dinghy with oranges and fresh water. Dad is nowhere to be seen. Bleary-eyed, I climb over the lifelines, tentatively letting down my toes until they find the cool soggy rubber of the little boat's floor.

As we head towards land, we smell the rotting flesh of coconut and the smoke from the village fires. I sit in my hooded sweatshirt, jerking back and then bracing myself and my coffee with each sweeping row. I watch the oars cut the still, deep water, lift and drip for a moment as they hover and the boat skims forward. Oars quickly slice again into the sheen, which reflects the light blue-orange of the sky, bringing my attention upwards to the white cotton puffs of early morning clouds.

We come to a slow stop, as the dinghy finds sand and slides gradually up the shore. I jump out too soon, losing my coffee in water up to my waist, but struggle to push the dinghy the rest of the way up to the shore anyway. Lucas smiles and laughs. He walks right down through the water to me, and his kiss makes my knees collapse. My heart hurts with pounding. I submit to him, his comforting embrace. We lay on the sand and look up at the sky for a moment, then Lucas stands with agility. I prop myself up, slowly finding balance, and follow him into the impenetrable lush green wall where the sand ends. Lucas cuts a path with each broad stroke of his machete. I follow, hacking at vines. We find more oranges, bananas, and guavas, and discover a clearing at the top of a hill that looks out to the sea.

Hidden in the hanging jungle behind us there is a village. We can hear their laughter and smell the smoke of their fires. I imagine families and elders and barefoot kids playing. There is wisdom, order, and cohesion. It is natural and simple, and that is okay.

As we walk back towards the dinghy, we approach

some fishermen in hand-carved canoes from the village. We soberly exchange stories, fishing techniques, smiles, and names of different fruits. Lucas can somehow speak to them in words, but I can also communicate, with gestures and facial expressions. I know they invite us to their village as I watch a small white bird chasing crabs on the sand. But, the roar of a motor flares like a gunshot through the quiet—Dad testing the engine. It is the summons back to the boat. We do not make it to the village where those wooden boats are carved.

When Lucas and I get near the boat, I see Dad is clean-shaven, dressed in a button-up shirt and shorts. He looks awkward, animal-like in stiff clothing. Anxiously he paces the small decks, stops to inspect a line, shakes his head, then resumes the pacing. As soon as the dinghy reaches the boat, Dad climbs in, takes the oars from Lucas, and redirects us to the other side of the lagoon, towards a river mouth. I think of the dress I want, tucked away in my duffel bag onboard, as I lift a vine-stained, calloused hand to my scraggly, sun-bleached hair. I want to be clean.

We pass the beach and the jungle. The coconut plantation is now beside us. The river we enter from the lagoon is encased with shadows and the scent of plumeria. Mosquitoes hum, and the water is dappled with light. We secure the dinghy to some mangroves and set out on one of the straight paths through the coco palms. The corrugated metal factory drips steaming ooze from burnt coconut flesh, or copra, as it is called. I see two thin, dark men working in that stink.

Behind a wall of bougainvillea bushes, the factory is forgotten. There is a manicured lawn that brings us to a long, whitewashed building, with proper beams and a clean wooden roof. Reminiscent of another era, of trading companies and British occupation, an old man sits on the porch of the plantation house. As we get closer, I can see that his white beard is yellow around the side of his mouth where the pipe was. He takes his time to stand, then welcomes us, with a puff, one hand in the pocket of his pleated shorts. We are ushered inside a dimly lit, high-ceilinged, hazy room. Tall, wicker rattan chairs circle faded woven rugs. Large elaborately framed portraits of similar-looking men with similar beards hang on the walls. Bar stools tuck up to a long shiny wooden bar that is warped and undulating with too much use.

As we saunter in, a few Australian men who own the plantation that supports the island sit at the stools. The plantation is a stark contrast to the jungle near the village. The organized rows of carefully planted palms have taken over the island, and the smoke from charred copra swirls into the air and settles low. I see a Danish couple at a nearby rattan table and I immediately go to talk to the woman. She is beautiful: her voice. Her mannerisms. Another woman comes who has lived here for years and raised her children in Papua New Guinea. Both women are interesting and inspiring. They tell me about the schools, the local markets. The best way to cook the fish. The rumor of our crew has traveled, and they have gathered here to meet us.

Dad reminds us that the tonic in the gin helps keep malaria at bay, laughing about how many mosquitoes there will be on the sultry river of our return route. So we drink the gin tonics, while picturing the massive production capacity the Aussies and Brits tell us about . . . the shipments and the men in the banking empires. The men with their crisp white shorts and neatly trimmed white beards. As the gin swirls through my head, I know the mosquitoes are still biting. The gin only numbs me to it. I feel myself fade into the background not wanting to be part of this conversation, wanting only to go to the jungle and village.

~~~~~~~~~

The next morning, peeking out from my bunk from under my sheet, still musty after drying on the line in the sun, I feel heavy, and trapped, in this paradise. There are diesel fumes mixed with the whiffs of too-strong coffee, and as I climb up on the deck, I sadly wave to the dark figures growing smaller on the beach, the jungle and the village I never got to know. The wake we leave behind undulates black and pink with the sunrise.

chapter thirty-one

solomon islands

~~~~~~~~~~~

Lucas is the first to see the land. He smiles and says coolly, "Ahoy, lads and lasses, paradise awaits us."

"You're just messing with me because you know I want a cold one, and a burger," Dad replies as he adjusts the sail to catch the quickened breeze.

Dad stands in the cockpit, taking the tiller from me, as he always does when we approach land. I scamper up to the bowsprit and climb atop the pillow of sails that are stowed in their billowing canvas bags. Here, I am surrounded by the sea to the front and sides, the boat and its occupants are behind me. I can hear only the rushing breeze, and the water parting to receive the bow of the boat. I can let my legs dangle, my toes dipping into the water after the boat crests a wave and I feel like I am flying. In rough water, I know I might be submerged. The bow could go down with me clinging on, then emerge free of my grasp forever.

Lucas stands on the top lifeline, between the two port stays, onto which he braces himself and gracefully balances. He pivots from the stabilizing stay cables, then lets go, as if he is performing a walk on a tightrope, gripping the top, tightly strung cable with the ball of his foot and toes. I watch Lucas's joy with a smile, but, turning to Dad, see that a stern sullenness has come over him.

~~~~~~~~~~

As our boat creeps into the bay, I know it might be the most beautiful place I will ever be. It is not that I can finally get off the boat and eat something besides canned food—the corned beef hash, the creamed corn. It is not that I can run on the sand and stretch my cramped muscles that have been bent into the square cockpit, or cramped in by my tiny bunk for several weeks now, or that I can clean my salty body, my hair. It is the light. The sun shines on the glistening palms and mangroves, and reflects off the water in glints of pale yellow. The water is clear, a magical hue of emerald, with orange and black striped fish flashing through swaying purple anemones. Looking down I see them magnified through the surface of the water.

There are lobsters down there, to spear. And fresh fruit on the trees above. My mouth waters. We all sit silently with anticipation as the boat glides towards the shore of the cove. Overwhelmed with the smells, sights, and sounds of land, senses quickened by the cleansing, yet monotonous, salty ocean air that we have breathed with only a few breaks on land. The first sign of earthly terrain, when you are out at sea, is the presence of birds squawking and circling over the waters, now shallower with reefs and teeming with fish. Far out on the open ocean, a visit from a bird is an occurrence that might happen once a week, and is welcomed like a visitor coming for tea or a scarce bottle of wine. The flocks we first come upon approaching this island are almost deafening, almost too much company all at once, after the solitude.

My ears adjust to the cries of the birds, and my olfactory senses are now readjusting to the warm, musty odors of approaching earth. These smells creep up on me acutely. Before land is even a shadow on the horizon, the salty air gives way to a distant smell of smoke that makes one pause; rumble of the stomach, heightened awareness of hunger. Hints of decaying foliage, cooking fish. In more populated areas, gasoline or exhaust might creep up the nostrils, and more garbage floats by. But here, an aroma of fertility, steeped in fragrant flowers, envelops me.

<hr />

Dad is at peace on the ocean. Mostly, people give him trouble. And land equates to people. Luckily, there are no signs of humans yet, no bars or ports or homes, so I know there is time. I want off the boat for a bit. I want expansiveness and freedom to explore on my own. In my mind I run through the inventory of what I will toss in my backpack as soon as we anchor: a machete, a tarp, some twine, matches, a pot, a cloth, my journal, a pen, and a book.

As the depth of the cove decreases and the sandy bottom calls through the clear teal water, our trances are disturbed. "Bexter, look for coral head, or reef! Lucas, prepare the anchor. We need some of that chain from the stern locker!" Dad booms, standing high on the stern deck with the tiller in his hand. I point to a large coral head at about ten degrees as Dad steers to port. I indicate with my hand to slow, as the shallow bottom looks good for anchor. Dad presses the lever with his foot and the engine shudders as it gears down and rumbles with a sleepier rhythm. Lucas has the anchor in place, the chain over the roller nest that guides it down to the ocean floor. I look at Lucas and we nod in agreement that it looks like a good place to drop anchor, and I yell "Dropping anchor" back to Dad, who throws the boat in reverse as soon as the anchor settles. A plume of diesel spills from the stern of the boat as she inches backwards, pulling the anchor and digging it in until the anchor line strains and the boat can no longer move. Dad cuts the engine. I am already inflating the dinghy.

As I row ashore, I can hear the distant, fading words of Dad and Lucas as they stow and tinker with their gear. As I pull away, I watch them and the boat grow smaller. The oars dip briefly into the glassy water at my sides as I skim forward, then I slice the oars in edgewise to press against the sea, away from Dad, as I pull the wooden handles to my chest. I see the approaching shore, a green intertwining of massive leaves, vines and colored feathers, meandering above the light brown sand.

chapter thirty-two

espiritu santo

June 11, 1993—Journal Entry

We arrived at the island of Espiritu Santo just before eleven
a.m. after a straightforward anchoring on a sandy ocean
floor. I was able to row ashore on my own after anchor.
Though I do not find fresh water to bathe, I find a liliquoi
vine. The sweet perfume juices drip down my chin and I
collect as many as I can in my sarong. When I return, we
eat ahi sashimi and I lay on the deck to tan my white, little
breasts in the sun. Lucas is asleep by the stern and Dad
left for town to take care of customs paperwork. My little
boobs are turning a light shade of pink. This is heaven.

After cleaning the boat, we motor to look for the yacht
club of Espiritu Santo to find a shower. Our anchorage
is in a lagoon. There are three wrecked old boats in the
shallows towards shore. From the chart I remember that
on land there are only three things that seemed to show

any sign of human habitation. I look for them now. I see an old shipyard, with more wrecked and rusty carcasses of boats. I also see two old, colonial-style shacks. This must be the yacht club. That is where we will land.

The air in Espiritu Santo is dense. Sudden blasts of it come out of nowhere. Still, heavy air, followed by a strong wind gust with no warning, almost like the breath of a dragon. Lucas thinks the place's name is eerie; it means "holy spirit," incongruent with its feel. Something is darker here than all the other islands, despite there being no clouds in the sky on this day. There is less sunlight. The air seems more dense. The people seem to hide behind trees, behind their homes.

We load the dinghy with soap and other toiletries and head to shore. "Enough of this saltwater douche, as Captain calls it. The bucket shower with sea water gets old. Too-cheap bastard, not to hook up hot water in his own boat, and to not even use the handheld shower in the head— what is that? Hardheaded son of a bitch your dad is," Lucas says, airing tension that had until now been quiet.

As we near, we look to shore with anticipation. We steer the dinghy towards the least dense section of mangroves and find an old dock near cement ruins. Lucas moors to the rusty iron remains of a post, and we scramble up the bank. I get my hair caught in a mangrove. Lucas can see the desperation in my face, just to get to the fresh water, as a chunk of blond hair tears out of my skull and remains hanging in a mangrove branch.

On top of the embankment, a lawn sprawls. It is wide and flat and the tufts of grass carpeting it are soft on our feet. "There she is!" says Lucas, as we walk towards the structure he had seen from the boat.

The little shack must be someone's home, but it is all locked up. There is a little canoe outside and inside there are drapes and a mattress. There is a structure outside surrounded by tin roofing material. It is in fact an outdoor shower, built with posts of bamboo, and sides of plywood and corrugated iron patched into walls. We pick up our speed, now jogging to the shower, like towards an oasis in a desert. Beside the structure, there is an old, rusted metal folding chair. Lucas sits down and gestures for me to go into the shower first. I lower my head to him graciously.

As I walk behind the partition wall, a chicken runs under the open section. I am aware that Lucas can still see my feet, ankles, and calves. There are bougainvillea bushes full and heavy with a deep pink on the perimeters of the lawn, and the plumerias smell sweet in the warm air. The layers of salt and sweat suddenly feel thick on my skin now that I know I can have a shower. It is fed by a rain cistern and I see that I am to pull on a string to release the water. The water is cool and tastes sweet. Soap feels so good. I am surprised that Lucas completely disappears when I take my shower, out of respect. Privacy. Nice to have clean hair and soapy-smelling skin. Fresh little dress.

After we both shower, I set up a sarong on the grass and work a comb through my tangled wet hair. Lucas breaks out his shaving knife and some soap. His beard has become so bristly and thick that he struggles to chop the tufts of stubble from his jaw. "Damn," he says slowly as he cuts himself for the second time—a hand mirror squeezed between his knees, littered with chunks of hair, working his knife with two hands. He stops as I look up at him, comb in my lap, hair better but still tangled. He offers the knife to me. I stand up and take it, brushing the blade between thumb and forefinger, and look at him with raised eyebrows. "How exactly do I do this?" I ask. "Are you sure I won't do more damage than you have?"

"Stand behind me, like that, and I'll lift my chin so the skin is tight. You just scrape the blade up, at a slight angle, and move my chin around so you get all the spots." I stand behind him and hold the blade to his exposed neck, as he looks at me with a smile. He trusts me. He respects me. I think I love him miserably. But we have to go home at some point, some next port, and my heart begins to feel heavier as time with him already seems to disappear.

The large grassy area is heaven to walk around in. A fire grill and cement slab with picnic tables and a roof are close to the plumerias. A swing. All this next to the beach under the trees. The tropical trees. And no one around. The birds and rustling trees are loud. It is like they are talking to me. While swinging I feel the beauty of the whole thing overtake me, my head feels so clear. Life is so simple but can be made so complicated. I love and have always loved being outside, cleaning and working and making a place. It is like when I was little, playing in the stream with other kids in Colorado. There we gathered food and put it in our sink and refrigerator made of rocks. We set up our rock chairs and beds, the cool water of the stream, *Cattle Creek*, washing us.

When we return to the boat we drink a stiff (for me) Bloody Mary and I make coffee. Lucas prepares fish. The coffee is good, with powdered milk and raw sugar and floating grinds. I cannot eat. The combination of Bloody Mary and coffee makes my stomach hurt. My body has been terrible and I am worried to be on the boat again for so long. First my shits are basically liquid, but now with chunks of what feels like rocks. I am getting cut from it. I am also having my period. It's not going well. My moon blood is wrong. A watery orange colour and it scares me. But what can I do? There are no doctors here. Dad will not help. Another gross thing, my butt has sores, little red spots from sitting on the hard salty decks all day and night. I am so angry that people carried slaves in ships across the sea. Crowded together. Shitting and puking. Where cuts don't heal and the salt water makes your skin red and raw. How did people do that? How did people survive that?

Lucas and I are getting agitated now. Hours have gone by and Dad is still not back. The fish is getting warm and old. We sit and talk. I fall more for Lucas, but I know I have to be careful. I have to realize we are two young people thrown together in close quarters in this romantic yet challenging environment of sailing around the Pacific. For months at a time. I'm so bad with feelings. And now I'm complicating them when it can just stay simple.

Dad is finally back with ice and he tells us about his ordeal. He was not in the bar as we had speculated. "I had to walk to town and deal with customs, who won't see me until tomorrow." Lucas cuts up what is left of the fresh fish for sashimi. He also makes steaks. I was worried before about what is happening with Lucas and me on the boat, but Dad likes Lucas.

We go ashore and cook more fish and eat sashimi with the two other guys anchored here, Paul and Cliff. Odd guys. They sailed from San Diego, where they met. They've been out here ten years. They told some good stories in the fashion of old American war vets. Despite their integrity, I do not particularly like them. I try to understand why. Maybe because they are coming from such a different generation. I don't feel like women are to be independent in their eyes. Nor the people of this place, "the needies," they call them. They talk about the changing government, which I don't completely understand. But it does not sound as though these guys like the idea of "the needies" having independence.

Spirits are heavy in the wind tonight. Little fireflies swirl. It is kind of a long, droning evening talking with Paul and Cliff and we finally return to the boat. Lucas and I try to fall asleep on the cockpit benches. "Such a little place and yet we're still so far apart," he says to me as he grabs my hand across the cockpit. I love his hands. Huge. Rough with callouses. Gentle. The spirit wind is loud and the rain sprinkles us despite the tarp we rig up. In the morning I am groggy even though the sun is all the way up now and Dad is long past getting laundry ready for me.

Later we go into town to check in with customs so that we can continue to cruise these islands. We get a ride in the back of a pickup, then walk through the town and go to one of two pensions there for beer. On the way home we stop at the other for more beer. I shop at the stalls for food and supplies, and when I am done Lucas and Dad are still in the bar, so I join them for more beer. We talk to some local guys there with dirty and ripped clothes. They smell like diesel. The people here are not nearly as nice as those in the Maskelyne Islands, I think. When I swim back to the boat, I am scared. Midway I realize how drunk I am.

~~~~~~~~~

Today is the third day of our sail. We still have four-hour shifts and Lucas and I are on. The hours just barely pass. I'm not too into writing right now, which makes it slower. But now Dad is all rummed up and listening to country music. He is on a high telling stories, which helps the shift end more quickly. This morning I take my shower before going to sleep, trying to hide my naked body on the foredeck and not get washed overboard while I try to fill the buckets and pour seawater over my head. We should all just be naked.

Dad catches Lucas and me cuddling together on the deck at about four a.m. Later he lectures me about getting my heart broken. So funny, I think, and I'm almost glad I can let go so easily. Now he is telling me about Socrates. Plato and the death of Socrates. "The fool doth think he is wise." Lucas is cooking canned curried chicken. I'm struggling with the tiller to hold my position and it is my watch, so I have no choice but to listen to Dad. No matter how frustrated I can get with him, a lot of what he says is interesting, funny, and wise. We have maybe seven more days.

~~~~~~~~

We have finally stopped off Guadalcanal Island. It seems as though we have been sailing for years and years. I want to go to land. Soon we will be in Honiara, the capital city of Solomon Islands—maybe in three hours, it is ten miles away. We caught a barracuda yesterday, on Lucas's twenty-third birthday. There are so many fish we can barely keep up with the lines we are trolling.

Sailing transports me beyond time and beauty, but I notice that I easily become irritated. Dad gets to me sometimes, that wonderful guy. Lucas and I are fine at the moment. I go back and forth between being completely in awe of him and possibly being in love with him. The sun and movement are constant and drain me, but it is so peaceful here. I have read *Invisible Man* and *The Collector* for my exams. I start *The Odyssey* and want to read *The Double* even though I don't need to for my exams. Reading goes well with being out here, if it's not too rough or wet. Propped up between the railings, splashed on now and then, and rocking and rocking. I retain every word.

I have thought a lot about my friends lately. I miss my little sis Sadie. Also I think about what I want out of life. What is my purpose. I want to paint and write to somehow share the beauty of all that I have seen. I want to keep learning and keep things simple. And still live in that little home that I've described so many times before—a small house with a wooden floor and big windows that bring the nature inside. A fireplace. A mountain, water, maybe the ocean. Being on the boat makes me less cynical and I even think more about little kids and husbands and all. I even play around with what it might be like to live with Lucas. He is interesting. Almost always working. We could actually live on a boat and sail, have a family, like that. I respect his independence and I guess that makes me feel comfortable with him.

chapter thirty-three

honiara

~~~~~~~~

June 16, 1993—Journal Entry

The land here melts my heart. The smell of the warm fruit
and other vegetation drifts to the boat and is calming.
We anchor for the night and cannot go ashore because
customs will not allow us to until we check in, which we
will do in Honiara. There seems to be a little resort on
shore. Small huts glow on the beach and colourful boats
are pulled up near them. The sea between us is silky black
and flashes with reflected lights. More lived-in-looking
huts with clotheslines waving pretty colours scatter the
outskirts of the resort. The beach is dotted with dark little
bodies. There are a few small fires.

A boat comes out to greet us and offer us water. We
must have come off as surly, Lucas and I cooking and
cleaning and Dad not in the most inviting mood. Dad's
extremism is challenging. So are his set ways. Yet somehow the humour on the boat is great. "Would you like
some ice with that?"

We have stopped making rice and pasta because something is wrong with the lining of the water tanks. Flakes of white rubbery paint are coming through the faucet. And we all puked when Dad made rice with seawater. It was like salty greyish-green slime that the white grains soaked up. We joke about the smell of urine off the back. This experience is beautiful, though I have to say I'm excited to get to land and get clean. To get out of this confinement and just go on a long walk. See new faces. Use my legs. Eat some rice!

Lucas and I have kissed each night on our watches, and I can't wait to cuddle with him in a bed. Clean sheets. With a toilet and shower nearby. To make love to him. But I'm sort of defensive about that because he is, I think, like me in our lifestyle in that it is common for us to just leave and go onto something and someone new. I really like him, though. But he might meet some other girl in a port along the way. What happens, happens. I could do the same. Even though I don't believe that for myself.

June 18, 1993—Journal Entry

We are finally allowed to go on land in Honiara, Solomon Islands, nine a.m., June 18, 1993. The town is large. Bigger than Port Vila. The people seem a bit more wild. We drink a beer before walking to the bank and customs, so everything seems surreal. But so many people seem messed up, weaving meandering paths as they walk—dark, downturned eyes, set jaws. I don't feel as safe here. But it is still beautiful and so are the people. We check into the Solomon Kitano Mendana Hotel. Dad says Lucas and I have to sleep onboard and I am pissed, but at least he lets me take a shower. Dad leaves for the airport to pick up his girlfriend, Freda. Lucas and I stay and make love. My knees are weak. His body is so powerful it almost scares me.

Dad comes back angry because his girlfriend does not show up. We don't know where she is, and even I am a bit worried. Lucas and I get a ride on a big aluminium boat back to *Cattle Creek*, but the drunk captain smashes right into our boat before Lucas and I can fend her off. There is a big dent in the fibreglass on the port side. Dad is not having a good day.

In the morning Lucas and I go to get fibreglass for the boat. It is fun to see the little kids swimming naked in the water and playing on the beach. And the people all hanging out outside. All the people I see here respect the Earth and have gardens watered by irrigation from streams. They use plants for medicine and clothing; ride bicycles and fish for sustenance; they make beautiful huts from palms and bamboo; and celebrate Earth's cycles— the moon, the rains, the tides, the sun. The Earth is a force unignored, unlike in America.

I am tired now. Lucas and I return to the boat and we do our best to patch the dent. He fixes the bilge, and I clean the inside and organize the food. We might be able to stay in the hotel tonight after all because Dad's romantic evening is shot. Shit, I hope she is okay. People are happily yelling and screaming and playing music outside.

June 19, 1993—Journal Entry

About 6:45 a.m. and I am groggy from sleep. I wake up so many times last night thinking that I am on the boat. Everything seems to be moving and swaying. Dad and Lucas and I went to the yacht club for dinner, the place packed with a strange conglomeration of different kinds of people. We meet a couple and their friend, all from the Netherlands. They are taking a similar route to Darwin. They tell us there is an island between Gizo and Darwin where we can stop and it will make the trip more comfortable! It is an island belonging to Papua New Guinea, though safe. New Guinea sounds scary. Women are not supposed to walk even in daylight, and people are warned never to leave their boats. Two boats have recently disappeared. One with no trace. And we are going. But the island they describe is an in-between island, one of the Louisiades, far enough away from the major areas of danger and also has no customs that we have to deal with.

Last night Lucas and I sat and talked and watched people. I was exhausted, so got a good, groggy buzz going. We talked about us being together. I tell him I am mad at how Dad can be. I am mad that he is interesting and charming. Upset that he leads women on. And sex. We talk about that. How it is fun. And for me, emotion can sneak in and I get scared. He talks about being lonely again. It makes me love him so much but also makes me sad. I am so happy he is here.

Before sunrise Dad and Lucas move the boat to calmer waters near the seawall. In the prior mooring, *Cattle Creek* rocked so much it was hard to stand. They leave me here, so I have time to write, and sleep in this little bed, and read. I am so content. I take a shower and make some tea, all the while listening to the tropical birds singing, smelling the tropical earth wake up with the warm sun. I want to paint today with the watercolours I brought in. It has been a long time. Also wax my legs. It has been a while for that as well.

June 21, 1993—Journal Entry

Several days in Honiara set into strange funky moods for me. Lucas and I walk to the market and find that later in the day, later in the week, the supplies and fresh greens lessen and only the dregs remain. We buy some beetle nut, something the locals wrap in lime leaves with lye and chew. It makes the teeth and gums red, and creates a relaxed state. It is a narcotic of sorts.

From the hotel, Dad and Lucas and I go to Chinese dinner, for a change. Our waitresses are feisty, flirtatious, and giggly, very excited to see two new men on the island. The alcohol costs more than half of the meal. At dinner, I feel insecure amongst these women, and just tired, so the prospect of trying the beetle nut after became exciting. Mistake. As soon as I begin to chew, sweat pours from my body. As I look into the bathroom mirror I see the droplets of sweat on my forehead form before my eyes. The walls and porcelain bath swirl with the red I spit out. Suddenly, I feel nauseous and puke. When I stand up black falls in veils over my vision and I feel myself going down. Lucas calls Dad into the bathroom and tells him I am convulsing. Dad puts me in a cold bath. It is terrible. Then, after about ten minutes, it all passes and I feel fine, just a little weary.

The day before we spent most of the day drinking. Started at the yacht club before twelve, after cleaning and wiping out the food lockers. Dad met an old man who drew us in. He and his buddies flew in the war here and are back for a reunion. He lives in New Mexico and studies nuclear waste. Because of this war.

———————

Dad's new girlfriend, Freda (the one he eventually moves to our little cabin in Colorado), supposedly called to say she was okay and just delayed, but none of us had gotten the message. She finally arrives and we now have an entire crew of wired energy. When Dad picks her up, Lucas and I go to the hotel room to make love. He always tells me sailing stories and holds me in his arms after. We are no longer allowed in the hotel room when Freda arrives.

We sleep on the boat, rocking, the rain patting the ocean deep in the night.

Today I am to go to the market and provision the boat. Clean, organize, load supplies. Gregg shows up out of the blue from Vanuatu as he was hired to move a boat from Port Vila to this harbour, so we have more good company. One of his crew members has malaria. He has a high fever and looks white. There is a bucket next to him filled with bile. He shivers in his sleep.

Being here I think more about the purpose of life. Not in a bad way. America can be so materialistic. Takes the Earth for granted. Here I guess it is the difference between respectfully using what the Earth can provide and then the balance of the luxury of civilization, which creates such a division. It is tempting and confusing, I suppose. Just find the good in it I guess.

I watch two Danish kids, boat kids, playing in the pooled water the ocean forms behind the seawall. Wild little ones. I like little kiddos.

June 23, 1993—Journal Entry

Violins seep up from below, though are not drowned out by the wind. I hear the loud voices of Dad and Lucas. I am out in the rain getting the dinghy ready. "Dinghy Girl," Dad calls me. It is one of my jobs. Our dinghy pushes through the water patterned with little bubbles from the rain. I have a cold. The cold that Dad and Lucas had that has taken me so long to get. Lucas is singing his "Becky McLaren" song that makes me smile. It is his last name. We have our own little culture and beauty.

Finally, in Honiara, we go on a tour inland. It is dry inland, and hot. The rain somehow stays over the ocean. We see the memorials where little children run out to greet us wearing war helmets and holding bullet shells from the fight on Bloody Ridge. We see an old warplane and the sunken ships from battles here in 1941 and 1942. A pilot of one of these planes is on a return visit and stands next to us looking at his plane. He is somewhere else in his mind.

Lucas and I follow brown kids with burnt-orange shocks of hair up to a field. "Come, mistas!" they call, scampering up the path, picking up bullet shells still scattering the ground under the tall dry grass. They bring them to us like treasures as they lead us to the top of the hill. An old plane wreck lies crumpled, overgrown with weeds, butterflies flitting about. The weight of a reality of planes flying overhead, dropping bombs, some fifty years ago during the Guadalcanal Campaign in which Japan and America play tug-of-war over an airfield, spraying bullets and who knows what else at this pristine environment, these peaceful people, makes my stomach churn.

A wide-eyed boy grabs my hand saying, "Look look, mista!" He gestures to the old military helmet he wears, dirt caked on one side, lilting too big on his little head with a weight he should never have to bear.

We meet a man named Ed, whom we spend some time with. I am embarrassed by the last evening we spend with him because we are all so drunk. We are not inconspicuous among all of the quiet and dignified people. Lucas and I go out with Gregg after we all get kicked out of the yacht club and end up swimming in the hotel pool. On the boat we get high and I am wet and cold and out of it. We decide to sleep on the foredeck. Lucas wakes me up and I shiver and am spaced out, so I have this cold now.

I am too nice for Lucas, we decide. He agrees. Which is bad. Bad. It is true. But now I can even drink on our sails, despite my propensity to seasickness. We have been out for a few days again, on our way to the Russell Islands.

I can drink on this passage. I can actually drink anywhere now! Yes, I have learned well.

Freda is sleeping down below. I hope she is okay. This boat is not for everyone. I've opened James Joyce's *A Portrait of the Artist as a Young Man*. I am excited for this sail, and Joyce's adventure.

chapter thirty-four

russell islands

~~~~~~~~~~~~~~~

June 26, 1993—Journal Entry

Dad pisses me off saying "You are so great!" He only says it when he is drinking. It makes me feel like he has to say it to cover what he really thinks of me. Stop stop stop, I think, wishing he could hear me. We arrive the day before at the Russell Islands, where we anchor at a pretty, modern village. All day we stay on the boat and catch up on sleep and read and speak to all the little children who come out on dugout canoes to visit. Lucas and I go snorkeling with them. I see sharks swim by. I get a bit scared but try to act calm. There are so many my breathing is off, but I regulate it by the fear. When I look up I see that the boat is so far away, my breathing gets fast and broken. I have to ask the little boys if I can get into their canoe. They nod no, but already I am trying. I almost get in, then I tip them over. Them and all the fish they have gotten for their family. I am such an idiot, but they laugh and swim around to gather their harvest and supplies that are floating off and sinking. With Lucas I feel safe, but my fear of sharks and the water is deepening to a desperate level.

Now we sail to a smaller island with no people. Lucas and Dad are now like bickering little kids arguing about how to traverse through the reef. I just braid my hair in little braids. It looks silly, but it is out of my eyes and can't so easily get tangled in the lines. My camera is out of batteries—this is so beautiful.

June 27, 1993—Journal Entry

At Nono Island, we recuperate. The sail in was tedious and we were all tense and annoyed with each other. Lucas and I go snorkeling and then later that night dive. I have a new technique of putting on my mask and staying in the dinghy so my body is not submerged with the sharks. Nighttime I get all the way in. Maybe because I cannot see the sharks so well, or that I feel one with them. The night water is so peaceful, but eerie and quiet. Lazy fish floating about. The water is so still. Lucas spears something. The spear trails a glow of plankton behind it. He hits his target, and then another fish. Then I know we are trailing blood with our catch, so I climb into the dinghy. Lucas tosses the catch in the dinghy at my feet and the spine of one of the fish sticks me in the toe, under the cuticle, and it hurts like hell. There must be poison in the spine because of how it burns, for at least two hours. More and more to be afraid of in these deep, dark waters. Lucas also gets big clams for bait. They glow blue in the night. When we get back to the boat it pours rain. I stand free and naked on the foredeck relishing the freshwater shower.

Sailing into Marovo Lagoon I feel sick all day long. Nauseous. Something I ate or all of the rum or something. Arriving here cures it. Small islands everywhere within the lagoon. The thatched houses are on stilts just beyond the beach in the trees. This morning, mist is coming down from the mountains to the little houses. The sun from yesterday is resting and the rain is washing this little part of the world. Lightly blowing breeze. Lingering in the clouds and mist. Occasionally spilling in a downpour.

It is time to bring the boat to anchor after three weeks of stifling heat. It is the last leg of the journey, with not enough breeze, so we have to motor. The seas are calm, which means it is okay to drink rum. We finish preparing for anchor, and I rush through my work, cleaning the dank motor oil that has sloshed though the companionway. I know I have to get out to this island, immediately, and I do. Because the movement will feel good to my atrophied legs. I love when my legs ache and are flushed red-hot with new circulation of the youth they are supposed to feel, when my heart pounds with sudden exertion. And because I just need to get away. I sleep on the island, under the stars.

In the morning Lucas goes to fish, Dad and Freda go running, and I walk around the island. It is so quiet. Every little sound stands out. Everything is alive and moving. I walk for a long time on the beach then find a little road and run a long way before I stop. It is a coconut plantation with a few cows roaming about. I get an eerie feeling reminding me of the plantation bar. Knowing there used to be jungle here. And probably a village.

The straight rows in which the coconut palms are planted extend out from where I stop running, feeling a bit lost. Wide spaces between each tree become narrower as they recede farther into the distance. The row of palms in front of me a perfect line, in which each tree hides precisely behind the next, progressively getting smaller and smaller, reaching a vanishing point I cannot, but want to, see. Slowly spinning around, I wonder how far the trees extend.

A mosquito lands on my forehead, and another on my arm. My belly and head swim, confused by the solid ground below my feet, after the constant rhythmic, bobbing roll of the little sailboat. Knowing I have to move to avoid the little stinging insects, and to quell my dizziness, I take a step, trance-like, feeling lost and small in that too big, too perfectly laid out geometric maze of the palm plantation. The sense of vertigo subsides as I pick up my pace to resume my jog, regretfully turning back in the direction from which I came. I want to continue deeper into the island, to the real island, but am unsure of this unknown place, alone. I feel oppressed by the too close, too old, too tall palms, desperately clinging to what shriveled brown coconuts they still manage to produce. The stringy, brown, withered fronds shade the still-blaring sunlight and heat from the fading day. I know there is lush green at the end of each row, but it seems impossibly far away. I feel weak in my choice to run back. I run faster, retracing the footprints made by my modern rubber-soled running shoes in the fine sand and dirt on the path that seems to have been, until then, strangely undisturbed.

As I retrace my tracks and near the bay, I notice with admiration that the boat still looks proud. The small wooden bow lightly bobs, and is silhouetted by the perfect, untouched crescent of white sand and lingering tropical green that droops and lounges against it.

Lucas sits on a quiet rock, hair wet, back glistening with droplets of water drying on darkly tanned skin. The clean smell of soap surrounds him. I would not normally have seen him there, but have developed another sense with this time on the boat. He cannot startle me like he used to. He looks up with his sly, flashing smile, still cleaning his nails with his pocketknife, gesturing his head towards the imprints on the sand by the water. A crocodile had sunned here too, the mark of his belly, his claws, and a line where he must have pulled his tail towards the bushes. I look at the bush questioningly for a brief moment. Then am drawn back to Lucas.

I love him there, like that, away from the geometric maze of the old coconut palms, on the sand where the crocodile sunned. But the fear, and feeling of confinement, does not go away with that love. I know there is something more.

<hr />

Lucas continues to the mangroves to pick oysters that cling to the roots. I help. He climbs coconut trees and we drink the juice and eat the soft meat.

When we return to the dinghy, Freda and Dad are lying on the beach. They are with two local guys who have huge welts on their ankles, which they scratch to open sores. One, Kevin Hoi, Marulaon Village, Russell Islands, gives me his address and he wants me to write. We cook the oysters over a fire and pound the rest with rocks so we can eat them raw. Pretty good. Eventually all the alcohol is consumed, and we are all singing and dancing and telling stories. The two men with the infections are half propped up on the sand, sloppily passing the bottle of rum back and forth, between giggles and drools and unabandoned scratching. I don't know if these guys have ever had alcohol before. Dad asks us to go to the boat and get food, beer, vodka, and Sambuca. And medicine for their open sores.

As we row the dinghy back to the boat, a canoe follows our wake. The men, urgently wanting to show us something, boldly grab onto our dinghy as Lucas and I climb aboard *Cattle Creek*. I look to where the first man is pointing and see the same red, inflamed welts on his feet and ankles. It looks like worms. Raw, open, and oozing where he has scratched. His friend has the same up the back of his calf and knee. Their eyes desperate, they plead for something to stop the itching, ripped flesh, and the infection. I go below to the first-aid locker to see what I can find.

"Pretty sparse. Maybe this ointment will help." I always talk to myself, under my breath. Emerging to give them the ointment, my stomach sinks as I see Lucas also hand them a bottle of rum, as God would hand down a magical elixir as a cure. The rum will help their scratching, and I pray the ointment kills the worms. We have to push their canoe away as they cling to *Cattle Creek* with desperate gratitude. They hesitantly paddle away and disappear into the mangroves.

On the boat, we tear off our clothes and do flips and dives off the deck. When we settle down I head back up to the bow, my refuge, with a bottle of wine to watch the stars fall and swirl. I am taken out of my reverie when Lucas pours the bottle over my head because I do not know where his tobacco is. I push him in the ocean, which shocks him because he is so strong.

The next day we are anchored in Marovo Lagoon and as the sun begins to rise on the glassy water, we are barraged by locals wanting to trade. They have intricate carvings with turtles, dolphins, eels. They use ebony, rosewood, and coconut wood. Their trade is themed by "spirit of the Solomons," which represents seventy-two demons that King Solomon captured and kept in a brass vessel and then threw into the sea. When the vessel is discovered and opened, the demons are set free and return to their home. So, images and talismans of these spirits are very important for the locals to share with us. And they want to share their nusa nusa (islands) with us. Trading is difficult and interesting. It is a fascinating way to see the nature of people.

Watching Freda laugh and Lucas smoke and talk with these beautiful people makes me see how amazing this life is. Dad is happy today. I like to see him happy. He bought a carved pig tusk for his necklace. He's got his rum and "staminade," an electrolyte drink, and his Loretta Lynn and Conway Twitty playing; it all makes him smile.

Always drenched. We are always wet it seems. I remember writing of my love of water and this trip is truly a test of that love. On our watches getting up and climbing into the moldy wet weather gear to sit and try to stay awake in a sort of nauseous daze—it is hard. Dad is telling one of his roundabout stories of Port Klang and Malaysia and the characters he met. He tells about their hunting and gathering and the men that can smell the tigers coming.

A man named John Wayne comes out on his canoe this morning. He wears a headdress of Ti leaves. His presence is royal and Lucas welcomes him well. Lucas and his family met and dove with him when they were last here on their boat, *Tevaké*. John Wayne remembers Lucas and his dad, Mr. Peter, as do some other locals. Some little kids paddle by. They are curious and want to stare at us and see inside of our boat. So beautiful, their faces, and their mannerisms and posture. A group has gone to find fruit and crayfish for us. We give them clothes, food, pens, and lighters in return. Another boat is here from Australia. Again a crew member has malaria. Malaria is bad here. One out of four people apparently gets it. Which one of us is going to be the lucky one?

Back on the boat, Dad is already entertaining a small audience of quiet, open-mouthed young men with sun-bleached, frizzy hair and dark, strong bodies. More of the villagers appear from nowhere, skimming silently across the glossy lagoon. Their small wooden canoes now forming a half circle about the boat. Some dare to touch the handrails, but most keep a safe distance.

In the evening more people continue to visit and trade. I trade my flowery sundress for an ebony shark pin that I can stick in my bun to hold my hair in place. Lucas and I get into a canoe and paddle around. We go to a river that one man tells us about. We walk along a path with orchids and green everywhere. The houses all have little rocks surrounding their paths and gardens with natural flowers and herbs, and small communal cooking houses off to the side. These bamboo homes last eighty years. All natural and handmade. They last longer than some of the cheap houses in the States. Also, these little kids carve their own canoes. Some of them at four years old. They fish and provide food for their families. If a mother pushing her four-year-old in a buggy in the United States saw this she might freak out.

The river has a magical quality. Everything is beautiful and I need a new word to describe it. Sweet water. I'm so thankful there are places in the world like this. Quiet and spirited and natural. A woman walks by with her dog. Her hair is wild, her face wrinkled like tanned leather. Her woven pack brims with roots. She walks by so quietly and at first I don't even notice her, but her smile calls to me in welcome. Further upstream Lucas is turned back because we have entered the area of the river that belongs to the women. Lucas goes to where the men wash. This is where we wash our skin, our hair, our clothes. Our souls. It is heaven to swim in this fresh water. The dappled sunlight decorates our hair. Young girls balance on rocks like otherworldly creatures. It reminds me of my introduction to the moon on that first sail on my mom's lap. The sense of being held, guided. The vines drip down from the vast trees connecting the water to the sky. This memory will never leave me.

I am grateful to Lucas for allowing me this time. So patient. As we walk back from the river, I lead us off track but he gets us right back to the beach so we can see our boat. Usually I can find my way anywhere in the mountains, or snow, in the wilderness, in the tropical jungle. I think I want to get lost here. Still, I follow Lucas. I wonder how many people really can go out and deal with bare nature anymore without all the funny equipment to polish it up. I want to spend more time like this with Lucas. But he is seeing this terrible, bitchy side of me that I let out towards Dad. A side of me that I hate.

Dad pisses me off because he ignores me, my needs. He can be so disrespectful and unknowingly hedonistic and chauvinistic, and I cannot help but want to fight it even when he is right. I need to be careful about how I act with other people. Also I have a hard time with Dad's praise of everything that is strange, different, or dysfunctional. I think he is full of shit sometimes in what he says to me.

Dad's mood sort of fades with the alcohol. It numbs him and his smile into sarcasm and bitterness. It makes me sad. But we all go to John Wayne's house. He gives us a carving and tells us about his fourth-generation grandfather who was a headhunter here. He tells us of the shrine where the skulls still perch and where the many old gods are worshipped. He says we cannot tell the secret, because there is only one God. The Seventh-day Adventist God, who was established by persistent, good-souled missionaries in 1914 or something. John Wayne built his house for these missionary guests who wish to study the culture.

I hope it does not rain again tonight because it is stagnant and crowded inside this boat. In the night I wake up with a bitterness buried in the hollow of my back and deep in the back of my throat. I am angry in the morning when I wake. Angry with Dad, angry about material things, confused about the confrontations the headhunters and missionaries must have had. Angry about the gaps between what I have gotten from what society can teach me and what is real in places like this. I am angry about Dad's obstinacy and angry that it even bothers me. It is naive obstinacy in a way, and beautiful at that, because it has gotten him places that a lot of people don't go. In his mind and in this world. He does his own thing his own way even when it does not fit with how others do it; he will not budge. People end up sacrificing for him. Or maybe that is just because I feel like I do. Maybe it is all in my mind. He is extremist and if I want to experience the beauty he brings to me with his life, I think I have to sacrifice.

I believe I have to sacrifice things like being comfortable. Sleeping and eating well. Basic things like being clean. I know it does not have to be as difficult as he makes it. It doesn't have to be as base. It can be beautiful like it is at the women's river. But that is not my home. I tell myself that just because I am struggling does not mean that it's really that difficult, and I know humans can adapt to almost anything.

And money. His girlfriends and money. Freda makes fun of me when he lets me use his money. It's a good competition: who is more respectful of his money. I don't give a shit because I'm working my ass off for both of them. When I'm not around him I don't get his money. I pay my own rent and bills and buy food from work. But still she mentions it, and it bothers me. It pisses me off because she gets nice things living with him—like his house that he finally decided to make nice when she moved in. The dinners, this trip. I do care about some of the nice things he has. From his grandparents. The things that tell a story about culture and history are irreplaceable—the old carved trunk, the silk scarf and things from their anthropological digs. The things to remember our family by.

June 29, 1993—Journal Entry

I now have a little carving of a squid, a flower, and a coconut; scribbled addresses from our friends. The men with the canoes now have a tube of ointment, a pocketknife, and a T-shirt that says "Save the whales," and probably also a headache. They have a way to reach me, if the mail can squeeze through the line of the horizon.

We are at sea again. The impossible blue of the deep ocean holding us. Flying fish scooting over our bow. The clouds move by in their unique shapes; cumulus bringing the rain from the east, the cirrus showing us the direction of the high-altitude winds. The waves formed by the current racing those formed by the wind. Lucas sits on the bow, grinning calmly, with the next port in his eyes. Dad sings as he examines the charts, pouring a thumb of whisky. I pick up the salted, wet anchor lines to be coiled and stowed.

At about three p.m., again the wine bottles open and the rum is brought out. Dad gets shit-faced. He is incredible but hard for me to deal with. So happy when he is leaving port. Talks and talks and laughs. Doesn't quite let you get a word in edgewise. Then as soon as we arrive anywhere, he is pissy. But hey, what can I say, he is beautiful. He is with God, as he says.

Bach plays into the night. I listen and wonder how much goes into making that classical music. How it can create the feelings in your heart, like love, like pain. The stars are out and the plankton glow like fire again. I don't even feel nauseous. What a difference it makes not to be seasick.

Everything seems so clear on the boat, looking out at the ocean. That long thin line of horizon where the sky meets the water and bursts forth with ever-changing colors and light. There is no choice but to be in this moment. But how to find the wisdom to live in the strength of what the horizon holds right here, right now, in each and every moment.

Lucas loves the sea. Sometimes it is difficult for me to watch him because I know he will always be lost in the sea. And he has so many stories. The things he says: "Just look at the horizon go there, rotating into infinity before us and forever." I worry, though, because he tells me that he is sad and lonely. That is hard for a person. He just came up here and I am embarrassed because of my naked, though now tanned, boobs. I am still wearing my magic necklace made from the shells we found in the Maskelyne Islands and my skin is brown everywhere but where it lays. He traces it with his fingers, we kiss and cuddle. I am sailing in the South Pacific.

Our watches have changed to three-hour shifts, from nine p.m. to midnight and three a.m. to six. At around four this morning we find a fish has bitten. Lucas pulls in a forty-five-pound ahi. Sort of hard to get it in the boat, but he gets it and hits it on the head with a winch handle. The cockpit is full of blood. I fall in love with him again. He tells me he thinks he is falling in love with me when he is drunk as we go to sleep after our first shift. I usually blow that sort of thing off, but it actually sort of means something to me for once. Scary. So we get all the blood and scales cleaned up and what is left is love.

chapter thirty-five

deep dive

~~~~~~~~~

Freda, Dad, and I get invited to go scuba diving. I went in a pool once. That was good enough for Danny, our guide. A quick briefing on the oxygen tanks, the regulators—which hand to hold them with. "Breathe slowly, consistently," he tells us. A metal speedboat purrs from the dock then skims with speed to more open water. Water still shallow and glistening with seagrass and coral, undulations of slight sand hills. The boat slows, water glassy, clouds wisp through the sky, and little mangrove islands dot the horizon. He tosses the anchor off the bow, paying out the chain, then reverses to secure us. He pulls out the oxygen tanks with backpack straps as we find our flippers and masks. A bit of direction then over the side.

He takes us down thirty meters the first time. It is so mesmerizing I almost forget my fear of sharks. There are manta rays and it's like I am floating in space. I love the sound of underwater. Slowed and dense. Popping with the movements of microscopic krill. We glide over swaying seagrass, breathing slowly. Eventually ocean-filtered sunbeams reveal a mass of barnacle-encrusted metal. And old warship, maybe forty feet long. Sand has pulled it under, and coral and sea creatures cover it, gnaw on it, to remove it from their home.

After exploring this ship, this relic of fear and ego and pride, the ocean floor slopes down, becoming more populated with coral heads. The colors break like glass and there are fairy fish. Huge clamshells with undulating neon blue lips. Sprouts of red anemones reach and suck and sway, then there is an edge and we descend, an unknown abyss behind us as we are entranced by the cliff wall in front of us.

Orange eels poke out of the tunnels and smile their sharp teeth. Schools of fish silver flashing. Subtly pink, large angelfish with delicately thin, bright-colored lines. I come out of my trance and look to my side to find Dad. I see a shadow. Breathe slowly. A shark passes behind me. I watch with embarrassment as Freda grabs another shark's tail. I remain still in this—the sharks'—world, in reverence. And fear. Though reverence more powerful. I see Dad way above me and slowly kick, knowing not to rise too fast. I cannot see the surface of the water, only cones of sunlight showering over me, lifting me. Out of a cave below reaches a tentacle, slowly coming out the small opening, then pouring itself fluidly out in its meandering form. Soft head and long lingering arms circling, fondling, and finally tensing and shooting up in front of me. I feel the movement of water and am left in a cloud of ink. I cannot see, my heart beats hard. I still breathe, though more jaggedly now. Somehow calmed, exhausted, pedaling my fins up towards the light.

We get back and work on the boat. Freda is angry at Dad because he was all over the Danish woman while we were diving. Lucas and I talk and laugh and dream about traveling.

chapter thirty-six

an island near port gizo

July 2, 1993—Journal Entry

In Tulina, John Wayne shows us another small temple or shrine with the skulls. We see a buried treasure underneath. Dad makes us leave Tulina so we can motor to another small island. We want beaches to explore and villagers to meet, but Dad wants to pass them all. It rains. All night. And we are stifling hot. Dad sweats this vinegary, sweaty smell that condenses in the boat along with the steam from cooking and the moisture of the rain. The odor of diesel lingers also. And we have to close the hatches so the rain does not come in. The mosquitoes are inside with us.

I am reading *Lady Sings the Blues* now and Billie Holiday's emotions linger in sections of songs that float through my head. I want to do something with myself. Continue painting or something. Just to establish myself. I may need to live alone again and recover like I did in college that first semester. I loved that time even though it was lonely.

But everything can feel lonely sometimes. And everything can feel alright. It just depends on your mind. I need to draw because I will lose it. And I just need to. Like Billie Holiday needs to sing.

July 5, 1993—Journal Entry

Now we are at Uepi Island Resort for two days. We convince Dad to come here as a last start before Gizo. He complains because there is no bar here. There is a little cabana where we can shower. We can also eat; there is warm rice and fresh, clean vegetables and broth. With my belly full I am content, and I find a small hammock far away from everyone where I can be. Something is wrong because my period is early and I feel sick. I have just wanted to be away and alone since this morning. I feel like a little wounded bird that wants to hide and get better.

Our first night here is drunken. We meet a couple from Australia who often come here with their two kids to dive. They own part of the resort and help run it from Australia. They show us where to snorkel in one of the most beautiful places I've ever seen. There are huge colourful reefs that drop off sharply. We see manta rays gliding below us as smooth as ghosts through the water. And sharks of course. I feel safe with Lucas and proud because even after a little boy yells, "Shark!" and excitedly flits around in the water, I get in and swim over to where the people are. There is a huge clam as big as me. The best is going far away with Lucas and watching him go in underwater tunnels and caves.

In the afternoon we play volleyball with the resort staff. They are athletic and graceful. At dinner we speak to the Australian couple and a man who is here writing a book on man's inhumanity to man. Lucas and I try to sleep in the boat. He rigs up the leeboard as a bed next to Dad's so we have a double bed. It is so hot that we end up sleeping outside, bringing all of the cushions.

But again it rains. We must have been a funny sight: two naked bodies running around, glowing in the moonlight, frantically trying to get down all the gear before it gets soaked. Lucas and me so carefree and natural even in the cramped, awkward confines of the boat. There is a strange distance between us also. Maybe because we are all living in such close proximity. It's a distance that he notices also. Some insecurity maybe. He jokes with Dad about marrying me and one time calls me his wife. Right now I tell him I would marry him to help him with his citizenship. That would be the careful way. The safe way. But it makes me question myself. Am I too spoiled and stubborn to be with him? He works hard and lives a sort of rough life I guess and likes it. I don't know that I can live like this for much longer.

The other night he was so cute because he asked me for a glass of water, but before asking said he did not mean to be chauvinistic, that he meant "please may I have a glass of water?" I often get so bitchy to Dad and all of these men about having respect for women because they make such a joke of it. I know it is only a sexless, personal respect that one earns, but I still fight about it.

Even here I seem to be waiting. Like this life is not real and something else is going to come. When I wake up, I feel like I should be somewhere else. Like I've just been watching and not asserting myself now that we are around other people. Around other people, I feel like I have to censor every thought that comes to my head to see if it is worthy of coming out. My throat always constricts and I remain silent. Instead, I put up a nice front and ask polite little questions that make me sick. Why can't I just have the confidence to speak? Tell funny stories and be a good conversationalist? I want to be fun to be with. I feel like such a bummer. But this is all so hard. Even though it is a gift and certainly is an adventure. I have been brainwashed to ask myself why any man would want to be around that; that a man deserves to be around a nice happy girl.

It rains all morning. Sex is nothing in life unless you feel strongly about each other and can continue a good relationship with respect. You can never be better than when you are in love. And to be in love you must love yourself. I can't see how anyone could love me forever, because I can't always love me. And Lucas is someone I think I want to love me forever, and it hurts that I don't believe he would. Maybe this disbelief is a cover-up from my questions and doubts about him also. I don't know yet.

~~~~~~~~

The other night we joked about just keeping in touch and calling each other when I graduate from college. I'm going to call him in December and see if he still likes me, and if I forget I owe him thirty bucks. If I call him and say I'm coming to visit he owes me the thirty bucks. We play Scrabble all morning while it rains. Dad decides to stay one more day, and Lucas and I might get to stay in the cabana! In a real bed! Being around Dad depresses me. He is a wonderful man, but his company taxes me.

Lucas says something I notice again. He is talking about when he found out someone close to him was doing coke. He made the metaphor of people being like layers of silt in the water and you never think anything different until water washes over it a little more one day to uncover something new and unexpected. Sometimes I feel stupid around him. I need to be alone.

I feel much better now that I have sat here and thought. The waves lapping on this little buggy beach have calmed me and my head no longer hurts. I'm reading Z.N. Hurston's *Their Eyes Were Watching God*. The sounds of the volleyball and laughter are tempting me, but I'll stay here a bit more just to become more clear and bright.

July 7, 1993—Journal Entry

Some strange mood has come over me again today. Last night was like a dream. A subtle mist fell over everything in my perspective to cover my mood. Maybe the moon had something to do with it. That eerie, full body that is a tunnel of light to another world, it sprinkles the peachy-orange dust from its hole in the sky. Overflowing most of it on the clouds which surround it and letting some of it filter through to settle on the trees and the earth and get into the eyes of people like me. My eyes are blurry with it and I am in a passive, happy mood all night. I listen to two kids tell stories at dinner then leave early to take advantage of my one night in a bed.

Lucas comes in late smelling of drink and smoke and asks me in his sly little way to make love. I don't want to. I feel uncomfortable and pissed like I want to crawl away. I think of Marvell's poem "To His Coy Mistress." I feel like the mistress who falls into a trap no matter which way she goes unless it is from her own perspective, and she can feel passion too, and not conquered. I don't feel understood or respected. Even considered. But I will, with reciprocity, some day, I then vow.

We motor to Gizo because there is no wind. We leave early in the morning under the crazy looming moon. I am reading today. I need to write on the books I've read so far so I can refresh my memory for exams. I have plenty of time to think. There are so many fish jumping beside the boat.

July 8, 1993—Journal Entry

There is rain again. Though now we are in the protective arms of the Gizo hotel. The funniest thing, I was playing with this darling girl here, Stenenka, and she loves hair. She wanted hair like mine and was playing with it. Her father, a very nice guy whom I click with right off, says that her hair will stop growing unless she eats her toast crust. I laugh thinking he is joking. He was not and begins to be very stern with both of us. Parents are strange.

Sex. Pleasure can be brought upon by yourself. I am still mad at Lucas. I don't quite recall anything that I can pinpoint other than him kissing my dad's ass and him telling me about this cheap older girl he screwed on his birthday. This sea smells intense and the rain is coming hard. We are in this Gizo hotel. One single and one double bed. It will be interesting to see who sleeps where.

We drink Bacardi all afternoon and I can tell I'm going to get angry. In a way I have had a great life and have incredible stories, but I feel selfish. I feel like a burden to these men. The rainwater is overflowing from the cisterns. I end up on the boat just to get away and I take a piss off the bowsprit. I dive into the ocean taking the risk of sharks, maybe even dragons, biting my ass. Getting sucked down by the centripetal force of the waves. I climb back up on *Cattle Creek* and she even seems uncomfortable being tossed around in the waves and being tied down by a chain. She understands me, understands that being swung around tethered at anchor and pissing and shitting and changing your tampon is all quite messy. It has to be amusing and finally I laugh. I laugh because I also have worms and I need to find something to eat that will kill them or maybe I'll just keep starving. I feel a sort of rage coming on, and *Cattle Creek*'s jostling and this rain feed me. The rain is pounding into the red reflection of the lights on the water and I hear the pipes on land vibrating from their overwhelming contents of water.

To be a woman is different. You can't walk around with an attitude here or it's unsafe. I have to hide my feelings and control myself.

chapter thirty-seven

the other world

~~~~~~~~~~

To make up, Lucas and I walk the sand, littered with palm fronds and scurrying with crabs feasting on the fallen coconuts. We sit to watch the sun come up.

"Why do you want to go back to school?" Lucas asks me finally. He sits cross-legged, tracing his finger through the sand.

I look at him pointedly. "What do you mean, why?"

"Don't you enjoy this? The constant beauty? The freedom?" He looks at the dunes of sand behind us, the ocean in front, and sweeps his hand around as if he owned them. "We wake up to this, or something like this, every day." I think he looks handsome with his hair sideways on his forehead from the wind.

"This is always here," I say, lying back and looking up at the sky. "Beauty. Freedom."

"Not when you have to pay for a mortgage, a family, have to go to a cubicle twenty-four-seven."

"A family is not beauty?"

"You know what I mean."

"Lucas. I want a future. There are possibilities out there that we don't even know of." I prop myself up on my elbows. "There are fascinating people who push their minds—we've met a few who come through. I want to learn from them. I go crazy here listening to the same thing all the time."

"It just seems like a prison." Lucas looks down and pulls a reed up from the sand.

"How would you know?"

He looks back at me, peeking out from a head hung low.

"I am sorry," I say. I know he did not have the opportunity. "You have something that so many people never will, and it did not even offer you a traditional education. But here you are, living your life and you love it. You are living the way so many people would only dream to."

"But not you?"

I sit up and throw a handful of sand out into the wind and watch it scatter away from us. "What about those other girls? Why do you want me here when there are all of those beautiful little things flitting around you? You think I am not looking. What is that for me?'

"It is freedom." Lucas smiles and tries to kiss me on the neck. I lean to the side so he cannot reach. "You know you are the one I love." He reaches down and clasps my hand in the sand.

I don't know what to do. My heart is fast and wants him, but I know there is more. "Do I know? Then why aren't you okay with my leaving?" I squint my eyes and look at the other side of the water. There is silence for some time. The wind blows the reeds gently, and they whistle softly. "I'll be back," I then say, quietly, as I squeeze his hand tighter.

Finally we motor back to the boat. Our stay here encourages growth within all of our relationships, I believe. Last night turned into hell. I went ashore and drank with the father of Stenenka. Thank God we had dinner. Lucas was in rare form talking with the kitchen staff. A teacher sat with us and it was fun to talk to him. I got pissed at Lucas and did not want to sleep on the boat with him, so I went out alone and he followed me. We made up and I ended up in tears talking about Dad and frustrations.

chapter thirty-eight

sail from gizo to thursday island

〜〜〜〜〜〜〜〜〜

July 13, 1993—Journal Entry

It is our fourth day out and I'm going crazy already. The first three days I am sick and cannot keep anything down. Yellow bile, warm fluid, from my mouth to the sea. In the night when I wake up there is water dripping on my legs. A lot of water. The end of the bunk is soaking wet as well as the flooring and counters. I don't want to wake up because it's my time to sleep, but I have to clean the water up. It is warm and mixed with diesel, so everything is slippery and hot and wet. It makes me more sick, and I'm throwing up.

I have to tell Dad about the water, but he is also sleeping. It's serious enough that I have to wake him up. He's the captain. Though I know he will be upset if I wake him. When he sees what's going on, he flips out. "At least you didn't get it on the clothes!" Dad flips me off. *I am the one leaking the water?* I think, confused. At least my stomach feels better when we clean the diesel up.

We convinced Dad to anchor tonight in the Louisiades Archipelago, thank God. But maybe it is better to just keep going to our next stop, like Dad likes, to just go and get it over with. None of us knows how long the rest of the sail will take anyway. I can't get a straight answer from Dad. I know from the chart this entire leg is somewhere around nine hundred miles. But it just took us three days to get 330 miles. Dad said something about fifteen days total.

Dad's been pissing in our drinking cups. We each have one designated cup and he pisses in them.

I'm so excited to get to Australia to see my little sisters. I've decided I want to live a nice life. It doesn't have to be much, just a little cabin to base out of, and a garden. Some time to paint and write. Maybe a dog and a cat. A few lovers here and there but not living with me. I also want while I'm young to travel. Where I can learn French and Spanish. Maybe Guatemala and then the French country-side. In my dreams.

July 18, 1993—Journal Entry

I want to get a quick word in my journal before my shift. The lagoon where we are is still part of Papua New Guinea. As soon as we see it my mood elevates incredibly. So happy to see land. I feel like I say this every time, but it's the most beautiful island I've ever seen. There is no one here. It's a bit drier and I get in the ocean and take a bath and laze in the sun. It's tormenting, this heaven versus hell. I'm so thankful to be able to experience a place like this. Not only no one around but the untainted beauty. The shells here are big and beautiful and alive.

Lucas is out snorkeling and almost gets caught in a deep coral cave. I keep trying to get crayfish. Then he follows huge fish, so I stay near him, and suddenly we are surrounded by three big sharks. If we had a spear gun he would've shot them so we could eat them. My breathing is too heavy. I can't dive any longer.

I walk around the island and find little huts. There are three little settlements and Dad and Freda are in the last one. We cook rice and eat out of coconut shells. I am making sleeping mats. I lay the mats down and sleep so well. There are no bugs or anything.

The boat has lost half a tank of diesel and water is still leaking. I have to prepare my head for this little trip so I don't get sick or pissed. This is the last leg, which is sad because I love the islands and the nice sails. It's just the drunken, messy sails when I'm sick that are hard.

I have a dream that Dad is shit-faced and comes to visit me at school. A guard sees him and beats him up terribly. I've never seen him in such bad shape. The school is like some strange tropical village where I lived. When I wake, Dad tells me he is worried about the Torres Strait, which is full of reefs and heavy current.

July 19, 1993—Journal Entry

Boredom or emptiness is finally nagging at me. Dad just told us it's another 815 miles from Thursday Island to Darwin. A flight might be the ticket. Sometimes this guy is a bit off. Though the weather has been nice and not too wet, and the days are sunny, I have been really seasick, which is just sort of miserable. I got down a small bit of ramen today. I could avoid the rough Torres Strait if I flew.

Yesterday we caught a mahi, which was a good meal though I couldn't keep it down. Dad was drinking rum and cut out the huge fish's heart. He held it in his hand.

We all watched it continue to beat in his palm. Dad became quiet, then he raised the heart to his mouth and swallowed it whole. Everything silenced except the creaking of the boat and the sea washing against her hull. He looked a little green and became more subdued after that.

I just checked the charts again for myself. Darwin: 1,237 miles from here, another fifteen days. Thursday Island is 425 miles from here and hopefully only four days. All I can do is pray that I can fly out of Thursday Island. I cannot wait to shower and see my sisters and eat pizza and drink iced tea. Thank God we have to stop at Thursday Island to get fuel. Dad's been using National Geographic as a chart for navigation. My fear of flying can easily be overlooked.

Lucas asked me to marry him last night. Funny thing. I am really not ready to get married. There is so much I want to do. I want to work. I want to paint and write and read. And live by myself. Live near my little sisters. Be near little Jeannette. He would be fun to live with though. A challenge definitely. He could keep me in line. But I don't know if I need or want to be kept in line. Have kids and an exciting life. Adventurous. Hard. Full of work. I feel like I would be locked in as a woman. Which wouldn't be so bad as long as I am free. Maybe all illusion. Maybe it would be terrible. No use speculating beyond a certain point. I turn my focus back to the sea.

The ocean is endless. Just blue waves, horizon, blue sky, and the clouds. At least it's blue. Dad's eyes are blue. Fiery blue. The indigo of fire just before it turns to orange with the heat. The icy blue of dry ice. The same power to stick to you and eat at your skin. I feel so much anger towards him. It is almost compassion too because I know he is sensitive. He complicates things. He's thinking he's keeping it simple, just like his dad told him to do.

I think about what it would be like to live all the time without electricity or refrigeration and no running water. It would be a drag. I feel like such a product of the late twentieth century and count on those luxuries. I just read Tillie Olsen's *Tell Me a Riddle*. She speaks of people suppressed by life situations and economy. How in this struggle even glimpses of art and beauty can be snuffed out and discouraged. How much can simple human strength transcend depression? I also have the poetry book which Emma gave to me. It talks about creativity and art. But that creativity must not only come from travel and experience, it comes from human strength. Emily Dickinson is the case in point.

I want to keep reading but my eyes hurt. I have a headache. And the headaches lead to puking. Never-ending saga. I want to read *The Hobbit*, but I think I will wait until landfall.

chapter thirty-nine

thursday island

~~~~~~~~~~~~~~~~~~~

The boat slows, water glassy, clouds wisp the sky and the little mangrove islands are a dot on the horizon. Lucas tosses the anchor off the bow, pays out the chain, then reverses to secure us. Bramble Cay.

July 21, 1993—Journal Entry
The evening on Bramble Cay I did not give justice to. Clear skies dripping heavy with stars. Warm, light breeze and no bugs. The only tracks arousing my attention were little kitty tracks. Wild little cats. When walking around the island I feel so free. In a little sarong, clean, aware of new sounds, and everything in sight. It seems that on the side of the islands, the southeast sides, not the leeward or windward sides, the coral comes right up to the grass and trees, bypassing sand. It is so soft and colourful and cradles imprints of other things once living, shells of huge clams and little creatures.

I find a stick cut sharp for husking coconuts and carry it as my little spear. At night, when the sun slyly sinks behind the clouds and lets the stars light like lanterns and reflect upon the calm ocean, I wait for Lucas to bring Dad and Freda to the boat. I sit in front of the little village thinking of what it would be like to be stranded here. This would be my new home. Could I live and sustain myself physically? More importantly, could I sustain myself mentally?

Lucas is zooming back and forth and strange lights are shining from the boat and dinghy, so I go up to meet him. "It's just Captain and Freda drinking on the boat," he says. We walk back and fix up our little hut and lay there talking and looking at the sky. We make love. I love his strong body and rough hands. How can he be so strong but gentle at the same time? I sleep and hear the echo of the waves deep from below the sand.

I have had dreams incorporating the movement and annoyance of the boat into life in Colorado. I am in the tower house feeling it shake and I look outside to see rocks tumbling down the hill. The house is rocking and throwing me about. I am worried and realize it's only the ocean and little *Cattle Creek*. Then I am sleeping under Dad's blanket and I can hear splashes. Though I am getting wet, I can't tell if I am out under stars and the ocean is splashing around us, or if I am in the house and it is leaking. I don't know what my home is, and if getting wet is comfort or concern. When we wake we must sail again.

~~~~~~~~

It is only the second day and I'm ready to stay out here on the ocean again. It's just this nausea that is a bummer. I cannot drink water, so what little food I do eat either comes up thick or chokes me. My body is drained and shaking. We have shortened the shifts, because they are hard. My little three-hour day shift is almost up. Then I sleep for my three-hour night. When I wake it will be dark. I love that time on the ocean. Will see what the passage brings.

July 25, 1993—Journal Entry

This boat is so terribly uncomfortable. It is beginning to wear on me. I still have been a bit sick and keep having terrible headaches, which makes the trip hard. We have been out for four days now since Bramble Cay. At the start this leg felt fun, but now only four days in seems like an endless time. The wind has been a bit high and seas a bit rough but not bad. We are just nearing the Torres Strait. The boat is finally dry and calm enough momentarily so that I can write. We will not go tonight into the strait so as not to hazard the reef's currents and islands at night.

Yesterday was exciting. Lucas and I have taken up reading to each other to pass the time. While listening to his story I saw a huge wave, so kept watch on that area of the ocean. Moments later I see what I call a big fish jump out of the water. It was a baby whale and some larger ones were swimming beside us and jumping way out of the water.

On my second watch today, I was trying to maneuvre the boat through big waves with some difficulty. The waves are strange. Because we are coming to a narrow passage of water, waves come from two different angles and the wind is up. I manage to surf down a good number of them; sometimes the power of the water pulls our nose sideways and the stern in and under so we are riding the wave like a surfboard. But a few times the stern gets so sucked under that both Lucas and I think we are going to flip. The cockpit is fully submerged in water. The question is flooding. Bags shoot across the cabin inside. It leaves me shaking and gets everyone's attention. After that we get the harnesses out so we won't be washed over like Lucas's book was—we cannot read the end.

The sun is hard and I am no longer enjoying it. I can't enjoy sleeping either. Going to sleep is hell because all I do is fantasize about food and being clean. My mouth is gummy and tastes of puke. Every time I go below and wake up, I feel terrible.

Lucas and I listened to the Steve Miller Band the other night, which was a nice little treat. He fell asleep in my arms, which made me happy though I could not sleep at all. Today we can see land! Australian land. Though it is still days before we get to Thursday Island. More than we think because of the current against us. I won't even count. Australian customs officials flew close over us today and we talked to them on the radio. I have been reading a good amount. On my watches to stay awake I review history in my mind. Also my English classes and my French. I am happy about how much I remember. Also it will help for my exams.

I am feeling afraid to go home. School has offered a new facet of living and I know that my reunion this fall will rekindle that. But now that lifestyle fits oddly with my life as I know it now.

July 30, 1993—Journal Entry

Last night was so relaxing. We anchored by little islets and cooked the fish that Lucas caught, in garlic and butter, and made satay onions. My mouth watered with each bite. Then we sat and played cards and drank Milo chocolate all night. I slept so well. The wind is up so high we cannot leave. We were going to take off at about four thirty a.m. but have to wait until the wind dies. It might take days. It feels like we are at sea at this anchorage.

Lucas woke me up this morning with a little kiss and crawled in my bunk to cuddle. We need to make love quickly and slyly as Dad and Freda are in the forecastle and the bathroom door is closed between us. Crazy horny kids. I can barely write the boat is rocking so much. It feels the same as getting up at five a.m. to ski at Mount Hood. That same strong wind and feeling of the power of the elements. So dramatic these things.

Dad spoke to the weather people in Australia at four this morning. Shit, I'm even getting sprayed on under the awning. Well, maybe I'll do something new and read all day. The rain is coming now. I need to go down below.

August 1, 1993—Journal Entry

I am down below this afternoon recovering from a morning of draining sun. It is beautiful today and we are close to Thursday Island. We slept well again last night. Our departure this morning was somewhat chaotic. Almost hit a fishing net when we got up at four because of the strange currents.

I am going a bit crazy. My mind is going wild with songs and books, etc. I am being a complete bitch, but the funny thing is that I feel so myself. I am a bitch and I ramble and I am so self-centred and judgmental. Also in this I am sort of sad. Though I hate it I also love it. It is getting to me now, but it is beautiful. We just listened to the Counting Crows and it made me cry. I am so sick of sharing time with people and then just leaving. I am going to miss Lucas. People are so incredible. Especially when they show themselves and their feelings, which is hard to do. And here things seem so alive. At home it is so hard to show self and feelings. I can never explain this sail to people. And compared to the ocean everything seems kind of jaded, like we live in a dying society desperately trying to find out where to direct energy. Lucas is lucky because he is so involved in the ocean; he has more of a direction for his energy. Myself I don't know. I'm sort of scattered, I think.

I hope to see Lucas again. He says he is going to take off when we finish in Australia, which is sad for me. I hope we meet up in New Zealand. Or hang out also in Australia. I am so excited to see my sisters there. I am having an incredibly difficult time with Dad because he really often makes me sick. But I love him. He is my dad. And I feel guilty. He has just hurt me, and Mom, so much it makes me sad and he still has not learned. I hope we make it to Thursday Island today instead of anchoring. Even if we can't clear customs I just want to get there. I want to go dancing.

August 2, 1993—Journal Entry

We pull slowly into the port of Thursday Island, a settlement of aborigines. There is always a strange, quiet tension when our boat comes to any port. I can feel it thick now. Tall, skinny people slowly walk towards the dock. One woman holds a baby. We all stare at each other, wanting to invite, but also weary.

Lucas and I jump off the boat before it slows to a stop at the pier. We run up the dock to find, instead of some customs buildings or boat club of some sort, a wide, well-trodden path of red sand. It leads through stilts that support small shacks made crudely of weathered grey wood. We make it as far as what appears to be the crossroads of the village, only twenty yards or so from the end of the pier, and stand, back to back, each looking down a wide, sanded path. Lucas looks on to a group of men at a card table. I see a woman leaning against a stilt pole of, presumably, her home. Her legs are disproportionately long, and her shoulders hunched down over her dry, blue-black-skinned torso. I smile at her, and she shyly at me. We stay there and in that silence there is so much. We have forced onto this culture a settlement, a reservation of sorts, removed from the vast timeless nature that has cradled its culture, its beauty and knowledge, through sun and drought, snakes and red dirt, throughout time, but not through mankind.

August 8, 1993—Journal Entry

I am adjusting well to sedentary existence on land here on Thursday Island. Our first evening was interesting. Incredible to be on land and actually walk around. We find a hotel with every luxury I love. There is running water, a toilet and shower, a bed. Food and fresh water. Our first stop on land, though, is a small bar. Crazy inside. Energetic people. The locals not knowing how to react to us. Then we come to the other establishment on the island and eat and drink. I get pissy and get in a fight with Dad and have a nightmare night. He tells me I am being spoiled because I want to sleep in the hotel, and that I just get pissed about everything. I think about how I so often end up doing his dirty work and take care of his shit, but I somehow believe that he is right. At least that is an anger left over from when I lived with him, and it remains on the boat. I hate him and am in tears. I feel pretty lost.

The next night I get even more upset because Lucas has a hickey on his neck from when he and Dad go out. I am pissed at him. We take the ferry from Thursday Island to Horn Island and barhop. We actually gamble at the first bar and Dad meets people. We eat and then watch a rugby game and then the lawn pool tournament his new friends play in. The group dynamics are interesting.

Lucas and I stay on the boat and have one of the best nights of sex that I have had in a while. Somehow I forget to be upset with him. The next day is good though lazy. I have to clean and restock the head and the galley, and the food lockers. I run for an hour in the morning. After, we play darts and laze around. Then, the family gets together to watch the movie *Basic Instinct*. We are all getting a little antsy now. The guy who runs the bar is nice. He has been entertaining for us. I love Australia so far.

Our stay on Thursday Island is getting a bit repetitive. The dust that rises and settles on our feet when we walk through the hot streets starts to settle in our pores and makes us dry and irritated. We are worse off in the hotel room as we are not able to get our three hours' reprieve from each other like we do on watch onboard the boat. We pick on Dad. Freda lays into him after the alcohol leeches up all of her sweetness and patience, and she tells him he is a liar. That he lies about who he is. She is actually all full of shit and pisses me off. No one can talk about my dad the way she is. Or my mom. She also speaks of Mom's boyfriends not being any better for us than all of Dad's girlfriends. So Dad is hurt. He leaves for the boat alone.

Lucas and I stay up and watch an Aussie film called *A League* and drink then go to the bathroom for some love. Freda, in ear range of us, the hate stirring within her, I assume.

I am not liking Freda. I have problems with her person as she is loud and rude. Always. She never shuts up. But that is something I can get over. I am sure I am equally in some distaste in her eyes. But then there is her position. With Emma it was good and whole and I was interested in her friendship and curious about her; I had respect for her, with room to grow. Then she is gone.

How am I supposed to deal with all of these women? A series of sometimes motherly, mostly not, feminine entities appear in Emma's place. They all melt and ooze into that same space, and now Freda is here like a hot, stubborn piece of old chewed gum.

Then there is me. I'm still angry and unforgiving. I have to watch that with people. My friends. I'm so set in this repellent bitch mode I'm afraid it will stick.

Lucas and I have a nice time with each other on Thursday Island at the end. I leave the boat in the morning, not to see him until we get to Darwin. I only give him a quick hug and kiss goodbye. I am so excited for my sisters to come. Had a good talk with them on the phone yesterday. Jeannette said I could live in her room with her, the little darling.

August 9, 1993—Journal Entry
Freda and I leave Dad and Lucas to sail off into the sunset and go to the airport in hopes of catching a standby flight. Who knows how long we could have been stuck here, but it's better than the boat. We are lucky to make the flight. The airplane is tiny; there are only two seats in the back and one other passenger, so one of us can sit with the pilot. Of course Freda said, "me, me, me," and piled her loud ass up there. The man next to me on the plane is nice and sympathetic. Tomorrow Emily and Sadie come. I am so excited to see their faces. Someone familiar to talk with and enjoy.

I just took a nap and a shower and am now sitting on the porch of the Frog Hollow Backpackers Hostel in Darwin, remembering the last few days. We arrived yesterday by a good stroke of luck. I miss Lucas and have yet to see how real my emotions for him are. How much my mind has learned to dramatize and fantasize my feelings. He can be just another person oozing into that hole. NO. I will never let that place be a hole. It can only stay a mountain to climb and I will never let anybody blow it to a crater. I'll just climb to meet someone on top, or maybe they are climbing to the top with me right now but the forest is too deep. I have not reached the tree line yet.

I am so thankful to be in Darwin. We take a little shuttle to the backpacker's place. Being on land and around these people is strange. I barely have any money, but other backpackers tell me if you order a drink you get a free meal. What a deal. A bunch of crazy girls come in and ask us into their crowd. They're on their final night of a three-day trip. Some guy invites us to a barbecue and we decide not to go. We hire bikes and ride around. We find the yacht club and then I ride out to some point and look around. It's so different looking out at the sea from land. I go to the tourist bureau and look at the pamphlets. I imagine a road trip to waterfalls and animal parks when Sadie and Emily arrive. I look for a small and inexpensive apartment for us to rent.

When I wake up in the creaky white-metal-framed hostel bed, I feel like I should be somewhere else and feel sad. Sad about me. There are so many beautiful people here. So many beautiful girls. I'm already scared for when Lucas comes. I hope it's okay. I'm going to try to clean myself up and exercise. I'm reading Toni Morrison's *The Bluest Eye*. She is one of the most favourite minds I've been exposed to. I love her brilliance and her feeling and the pictures she paints. I want to eat Mexican food for dinner and sit quietly on the beach and read, and watch the sun even though it already set.

August 15, 1993—Journal Entry

Emily and Sadie are here and I have been laughing since they arrived. I am so happy, I love them both so much. I have been a bitch to Freda, though, I must say. I need to get some of this anger figured out. When we pick up the girls and Freda's son and we check into the little apartment, I am so thankful for the shower and a clean place to dress and be private. We walk to the waterfront and find an outdoor food and crafts fair. There are street performers.

Freda has Dad's credit card and uses it to rent the apartment. We convince her to rent a car and I tell her about the trip I found at the tourist bureau. Driving on the left side of the road is a bit odd. We go to the wildlife preserve and see crocodiles and wallabies and kangaroos. We hike up two waterfalls in Chatfield Park. We swim in cool ponds. Something is wrong with my foot and walking is killing me. I can barely stand. Maybe I fractured it on the boat or something.

I'm having fantasies about Lucas. I'm scared to say this, but I feel like there is something good and lasting about us. I'm thinking of when I get out of school and what I'm going to do with my life. I want to travel and I want to get a job with art or English, maybe teaching to start. I'm excited to earn some money. I want to move to Hawaii and be with Lucas and maybe eventually fulfill that fantasy of kiddies and a husband and a loving family.

Emily and I had a long talk about our family last night. At night I have not been able to sleep well, so used to our continuous sleep and wake shifts. Freda yells at everyone we meet and is so rude. She smokes in this car we are all crammed in for hours. She is explaining to us the reason Dad and Mom got married was because Mom was pregnant with me. Then brings up that Mom has terrible boyfriends. True or not, she has no right to bring that stuff up as artillery. We cannot be in a car with Freda any longer and decide to go back early. Emily cries every time we talk about Dad because he is so impossible. Sadie laughs. Freda calls the Coast Watch because she misses him. Dad and Lucas have not been spotted yet.

August 20, 1993—Journal Entry

When they do get in, we had been at the yacht club and Freda had been drinking. She immediately attacks me. I try to stay calm and say, "Freda, I am sick of your manners. Who the hell are you to say the things you say to me? Who the hell are you to bitch at my mom at Thanksgiving, to tell me what I study is pointless? You put down my mom and my dad. You make scenes. You are rude to me and my family and almost everyone you meet." She is disgusting. Her mouth is open. I can see the gum waiting to be snapped again as she stares at me.

Lucas takes me aside and hugs me. "I missed you so much. I love you and do not want to be away from you so long," he says. His face looks pained. I ask if he is okay. There was an accident on their passage. He was cook, in my place, and when he was boiling water that balanced on the gimballed stove, the boat lurched and steaming water dumped on his waist, soaked his shorts, and boiled his skin. His shorts stuck to him, the scalding water on the cloth blistered and peeled the skin off of his penis and lower belly. He had to continue on in the moist, salty, sweaty water for days and it had not healed well.

Freda and I coexist, and I am so happy to have my sisters and Lucas. We go out and find music. Lucas watches us dance, and smokes his weed. We hold each other in the night. I love him so much.

Freda is supposed to take care of our travel plans but does nothing. I go get our tickets and transportation. The travel agent helps me for two and a half hours on her day off, with student fares and discount prices. I do not have payment, but she reserves everything for me anyway. Freda's son is at the apartment, scared and alone. I help him find her at the bar. She and my dad are drinking and she yells at me for getting the tickets. I walk away. Teary, sad, and pissed at this constant drunkenness. She calls after me to cancel the tickets, yelling that I made mistakes, and I turn, shaking, and I finally yell, "You do it your rude self. I hate you! Someone had to get it done. We need to leave here, you bitch!" It felt so good, my throat hurt. I don't think I have ever gotten angry directly at someone and raised my voice like that before. Dad and Lucas come over, drunk, and try to give me advice. Lucas tells me he could marry me.

The boat is tied to the old wooden posts out in the water close to shore so that the trailer can hook up to it and drag her ashore. It is a peaceful morning. Clouds. I wish it would rain. I wish the clouds would explode and drench us all and wash us all clean. The more I think about the thing with Freda, the more upset I get. But I am also worried about me. Lucas, I love him, but he is like Dad in many ways. I want to take my exams and do well. Dad is organizing on the boat. Seeing him gives me a sad feeling. It used to make me so happy and proud. Excited even. Now just sad. He told me to fuck off again last night. For no reason. I asked him to pay for the plane tickets the lady held for us and he told me to fuck off.

chapter forty

new zealand

~~~~~~~~~~

August 26, 1993—Journal Entry

The boat is out of the water now and we clean her up
to get her tucked away until the next voyage. Sadie and
Em and I have so much fun. Slaphappy and crazy and
dancing as we work. We wipe out all of the muck from
the lockers. Clean the toilet, which bubbles grey, putrid
liquid. We take all the gear off, clean and organize and
transport it to the storage lockers. I like working. It gives
me a purpose and I am doing something productive.

We meet a lot of people at the harbour and yacht club
and invite them to a barbecue at our apartment. We meet
Cameron, a young bartender who gives Emily and Sadie
and me as much iced tea as we want and understands our
plight with the drunkards. He helps us work and tells us
how he helps the homeless kids in Darwin. At our BBQ
we all drink a lot. I drink more rum because I know it
is what Sadie and Emily are drinking and I don't want
them to drink too much. Our party ends up at the bar

and walking home I am scared for Sadie and Emily as I know it is not safe to walk here at night.

When we get to the apartment the TV has been thrown out the window, and Dad's radio, our plane tickets, his money, my silver bracelet from my grandparents, my passport, and our beer have been stolen. First thing in the morning the police have recovered only my passport, with its photo razor-cut out. I leave for Sydney to get my travel documents so I don't get stuck here, and everyone else, except for my sisters who have to fly home, will meet me in New Zealand. As I travel on the bus, the planes, I am too distracted to read. I miss Lucas, Sadie, and Emily terribly. The consulate is so easy. The sky in Sydney seems so elegant, brisk, and beautiful. I get all of my papers taken care of and rush to the airport so I can hopefully meet Lucas at his gate. He is talking to a girl. It is kind of cute. I see how much he likes her. My heart hurts. He sees me and shyly says goodbye to her. We go to Dad's gate. When he sees us he says, "Oh no! Not you guys again!" Freda asks me if I am still pissed. Dad asks Lucas, "Okay, how serious are you and my daughter?"

Being in an airport this time, I feel different than when I arrived several years before. So much more free and independent. I feel like I have unlocked a cage I have been living in. Dad knew I was in there and never let me out. Now that I am he is pissed.

Lucas is worried about customs. He has no real country and is illegal. His dad from England and mom from New Zealand, they set off on a boat and never got him proper papers or visas or updated his passport. We make it out of the airport and Lucas and I take off to explore New Zealand. He tells me he loves me and will never cheat on me and his heart will always be open to me. His aunt Sharon and cousin pick us up and take us to a rugby game.

I have the runs and puke because my system is still messed up from the boat and so much alcohol. At dinner we look at photos of Lucas's family, their sailing journeys on *Tevaké* and articles his parents wrote for a sailing magazine. Dad would never submit an article like that.

Lucas wants to see if I can work in his family's art gallery in Kauai, which is exactly what I want to do. He is easy to trust and gets along with everyone. He wants to travel and sail and is smart and I love him. We get on so well and have been through so much. But, I feel boring to him. I am afraid I am not enough. There is some void. He loves that fighting, drinking, rough crowd. I have just been born into it but don't like it. I know there is something else. But I am afraid that I can't fit into that something else. I don't want to type people. Why do I have to feel so damn insecure about myself? My exams. I cannot talk in class. The vice grip that forms in my throat telling me that I am an imposter in that world. That I am not enough and have no idea what I am doing paralyzes me. Somehow I have to learn, in that world, like I finally have here, how to talk when I want to. Have a voice that speaks the strength I know I have inside. I need to get the confidence to do the things I know I can do, or at least try and maybe mess up.

We are lounging on the couches of the New Zealand public library in Wellington after a long day of walking through the city. We took the train here and on it watched *Once We Were Warriors*, a movie about the Maori. The violence and degradation. Strong women characters (some). How sad that so many cultures have just been, and continue to be, stepped on.

We go to thrift stores to find warm clothes. We get a hotel and take hot showers and make love over and over again. Later we go to his uncle's ship, *The Spirit of Freedom*.

He gives us a beautiful bedroom on the boat with a shower and everything. I've never slept on a real bed in a real room on a boat before.

The harbour is dark except for the lights of the city and the boats. We depart at six p.m., the misty air reflecting some sort of vibrant, mysterious glow. The ship moves like a glacier through the water, silent and powerful. After we watch her clear the harbour, we go to the bar to meet the crew members. There are fourteen in all. They begin politely and apologize for the harsh language. Then they get to know me and feel comfortable and they just let it flow. I take it all in. We sleep that night like babies in a slow-rocking cradle.

In the morning I wake to Lucas looking at me. "I want to marry you," he says. I instantly feel guilty and spoiled. I want more. I want to live a refined life even though I don't know how to do it. Now that I have broken a little bit from Dad, I want to experience more of life for myself. I could have that with Lucas, but I'm scared. He just holds me in his arms and knows all of this without my saying anything. We walk outside and watch the sun rise as we arrive to the town of Lyttelton. We disembark and walk around. I buy the book *Papillion* in a used bookstore. One of the crew members drives us to Christchurch, where we take a bus to Rakaia. From there we hitchhike to Methuen, where we are supposed to find Dad again. We find him in the brewpub with Freda and our same pattern starts up again. I get annoyed at the smoking, the drinking, the lack of manners. I just want to hide on the beach and snuggle up and read.

Today is sad. Our drive brings us to Ashburn so Lucas can catch his bus. I watch him leave. I see his back. It reminds me of how he says he's lonely. I drive back to Methuen without him and cry. I cry hard and my eyes sting with all the emotion and all the confusion I have inside. I smile when I think of how he would call the command "Wind in hair" when he would see me struggling to navigate on the boat with my saltwater-plastered hair in my eyes. And how he would randomly yell across the boat, "I will always be your friend!" I think of him on the islands meeting the locals. Especially the Russell Islands with the guys with the worms in their legs. Yelling when happily intoxicated, "These are my friends!"

We are both so confused by what we've been exposed to and by what society lays out for us. I don't like the fights and pot and women and escapism. I notice through my tears the hills dotted with fluffy spots of cotton sheep. It is a narrow, windy road going up into jagged mountains covered by the same blue mist that sometimes lingers above the ocean. There are snow-covered mountains, and then the ocean in the distance. Beautiful waves crashing over black volcanic rock that spray white dewy foam into the air. It seems as though fairies have carried the mist up to the mountains with the effect of creating a repose for all of the Earth and us. Humans are so strange. Lucas would love these waves.

The sailing trip seems like a dream. It is wrapped up in fine veils and becoming more of a distant, objective something in the past from which memories glimmer. Lucas feels like that also. I'm sad that we are so far apart from each other. I think we are so good together because we understand so much of each other. The understanding only goes so far. We need to accept all of each other. Openly but without sacrificing or creating a facade for our true beliefs.

chapter forty-one

college

September 22, 1993—Journal Entry

I get a partial scholarship to a college in Washington. At school I cannot bring myself to join the sorority. I am one of the only students to let an apartment off campus. There is a scraggly young woman in the little complex. I can tell she is doing drugs. She lingers near my door when I get home, and it makes me forget that it is hard for me to be around all of the campus people and listen to my professors and their interpretations. I eat rice and beans and cabbage and notice the beautiful colours they make when they boil over onto my rusted, white electric stove. My sleeping pad is against the wall in the middle of my room, with books and clothes scattered around it. I work at the coffee cart early in the morning and prep salads at a restaurant after school. I edit for the college paper. When I get home all I want to do is read and write, and I don't care that the scraggly lady peers in my window.

I am obsessed with all I read about, with what I find in the library, with writing, with painting, with skiing in the blue mountains and running through the hills. I am obsessed with losing weight and trying to look okay and eating healthy food and exercising. I can't help notice all of the waste. The markets here are so full of so many brands and choices I get overwhelmed, but I am also so thankful to not be on the boat and to have to eat canned fatty foods and drink all the time.

I call Lucas and he has gotten work in New Zealand. I wake up in the middle of the night and look for him next to me. I get up before the sun and think I am on the boat and struggle to find solid ground beneath my feet. All I can do is run. I run on the pathway to the river. I run through the golden hills. I go to class, I study, I work in the library and prep salads in the restaurant. I go to the bars. I still drink too much.

part III

chapter forty-two

big island

~~~~~~~~

March 2, 1995—Journal Entry

I am still a bit loaded when Lucas and his friends pick me up at the Hilo airport. We are dropped off and walk down a dark dirt path in the rainforest to a small shack. Lucas's home. It is about ten by ten feet with a small patio. Inside is a shelf, the shape of a square C, which acts as a bed, a table, a counter and a closet. He has a stereo, a light, and a fan. No water. Plywood walls. Corrugated metal roof that sings with rain dropping. Better than I thought.

We head to a BBQ with tons of people, lots of kids. There we meet Lucas's friend RA and begin a three-day blur. We go on a long, windy road through tunnels of trees to some old house of his uncle's. We smoke something in the car to add to the craziness. Something I have never smoked before. The house is empty, old and funky, natural and spirited, perched high in the trees on a hill just up from the beach. There is one light and we sit on the wood floor and talk for hours.

We wake up early the next morning and I wander to the ocean and sit. I feel like shit. We drive to some store to buy beer. It is eight a.m. I cannot drink. Another party. RA's family feeds us and lets us shower. They are descendants of a coffee empire family and have traveled the world. I am a mess and thankful for their gracious, kind care. We drive to another beautiful vacant house that it feels like we are breaking into. We smoke more. Stay up and drink. The next day is lazy and comfortable. Lucas and I make love and my body feels weak. I am floating on hunger, sex, and recuperating. Once we eat and feel normal again, we drive to meet Lucas's mom and sister. We end up at hot pools and steam vents and can see the glow of the volcano.

Lucas has a different lifestyle. He is so gentle and loving and treats me well. I guess he does not know how to treat a girl all the time, but his fundamental treatment is so caring. He needs to get married to get citizenship and I would love to help him out. It could work. We both want to do the same things, we get on well and love each other. I am just scared.

But here is not my final destination, in place or in this lifestyle. I am finished with college and Dad has invited me to sail with him in Indonesia. I leave Lucas and Hawaii to get on a plane and wait for Dad to arrive in Ujung Pandang on our *Cattle Creek*. I fly via Bali. I walk the beach there and relish the sun, the people, smells, and music. I walk through the beautiful women selling sarongs and jewelry and watches. Pushy but peaceful, confident eyes. I sit at a bar for a while to write and meet a local guy who buys me clove cigarettes. I don't feel scared here. I want to travel so much more. My feet are swollen from the heat here, but I walk back from Kuta to the airport. I distract myself from the heat and the sweat by noticing the beautiful buildings, the Hindu statues, and the constant smell of incense. So beautiful. So different. How incredible to have been able to be here even twenty years ago, in the mid1970s, before Dunkin' Donuts hit the airport. New York is more scary.

chapter forty-three

grey beard

~~~~~~~~~~~~~~

March 9, 1995—Journal Entry

In Ujung Pandang, Dad's friend Grey Beard picks me up at the airport. He finds me amidst a crowd of people who are sending their loved ones off on their pilgrimage to Mecca. That reminds me of J.R., from the Utah raft trip, his quest for Mecca.

Grey Beard is from Scotland. An old, cigar-smoking man who has a local wife and family here, and also one in New Zealand. But he lives in Darwin, Australia. He is an historian and teaches at university in Australia and Singapore and also works in museums. The drive with him is fascinating. People on rickshaws. I am driven to a hotel and my bags are carried in. This is much better than the working and lugging I am used to. My room has a toilet. Grey Beard, whose name I learn is Collin Jack-Hinton, will take me to the bank tomorrow, then to meet his family. I hope Dad comes in soon. There is no way to know. God bless him, Mom, and my sisters. And Lucas. If I could express how magical all of this is to me . . . I am angry with myself for not being able to portray the excellence of all of these experiences. I feel like something is bypassed in my head. My inability to speak. My fragmented sentences. To compensate I bridge with details and perfection. Pushing myself. I began *Anna Karenina* this morning and in the introduction Tolstoy writes: "Genius is belief in oneself and the importance of one's mission without which the energy is dissipated into hesitations and inner conflicts."

I know my mission and its importance. My lack is in believing in myself. My mission is to find and delve into the good in people and the experience of life. I can document it in writing and painting. And impart love and compassion because I feel like I understand. If only I could paint as much as I write, but time leads me to write. I will never have enough books or journals for this trip.

In the morning there is panic in my heart as I think I slept in. I dress and organize, write quickly and smoke, then go downstairs for breakfast. One clock says seven and the other eight. I am immediately approached and seated for coffee, toast, and a boiled egg. Collin comes at nine, so either way I am fine. Collin arrives and whisks me to the bank, a museum. We see megaliths of the Toraja Region, beautiful pottery, not studied yet. He knows I like art and anthropology. We have a beer, then go to his house. I meet his wife and youngest daughter, Geko. His wife feeds us spicy curry. Many girls, around fourteen, flock. All friendly and curious. They want me to write them. They want to take pictures. They want to learn English and I want to learn Indonesian. They ask a lot of questions about me. My boyfriend. Marriage. America. Religion. School. Work. I don't feel like I know how to answer, but they laugh at whatever I say.

That night a customs official comes to my hotel to ask about the boat. In the morning Collin rings to say a boat has arrived. I shower, eat and walk down to the water. There is little *Cattle Creek*. She is back home. Dad and his friend Bob, from Colorado, come in from the boat and they look completely dazed. Collin and I wait for them to clear customs. We find a restaurant where Bob orders a gruel, the oatmeal-like soup with fish flakes. He did not know how to order and was so hungry for decent food after the canned crap on the boat. Kind of funny. We spend the next few hours drinking and eating and finally get them settled into the Losari Beach Hotel.

I begin to explore for goods to import. There is a silk store. There is a region nearby where women weave, and Bob and I go there. The women sit on mats and thin out the silkworm strands into threads by hand. They dye it with magnificent colors with local roots and leaves. Then they weave it in their wooden looms. The patterns they create are meticulously perfect. We eat at the food stalls and I get used to the chunks of liver and fat once again.

〰〰〰〰

I miss Lucas and think of him often. When he and I laid on the beach looking up at the clouds, his hair reminded me of those peacock feathers that blend like chameleons perfectly with the sand. He loves to be around people. Everyone immediately knows him on the docks, at the beach. He knows where to get the best "grinds," and which shops to go to borrow surfboards and kayaks. Often I would notice him just staring into the horizon over the ocean. Or at the clouds. I would ask him what he saw. Without answering he would then come up and slide his arm around my shoulder and change the subject. Was that what it was that kept me connected to him? We had a history, but it seems we have so little in common now.

chapter forty-four

lee lee

~~~~~~

I sit alone in the corner of an open-air restaurant. Dad walks in quietly, humbly, as he has not had a drink yet, though it is already four p.m. It has been a long, hot day working on the boat. A small Indonesian woman comes out of the kitchen and smiles largely at us, pulling out a chair for Dad to join me, wiping off the table, bowing and gesturing with an open sweep of her arm in a welcome sign to sit down. Only then does Lee Lee look over at us, and I catch her eye. She smiles shyly then looks down respectfully, but I can tell she wants to keep looking, and so do I.

I meet Lee Lee officially at the end of the evening. Dad has become loud and friendly with the German men who are living there engineering a bridge in Ujung Pandang. I get up, bleary-eyed, to find my way to the restroom and Lee Lee jumps up to intercept me, placing a paper napkin in my hands. "Hello, I am Lee Lee. You will need this." Then she shows me how to tie the napkin into my hair.

"Thank you. My name is Becky." Feeling a commonality, the bar I guess, I look into Lee Lee's wide brown eyes and notice a yellowish tinge to the whites around her pupils. She is probably younger than me, but it is hard to tell. She has a kind, round face, is shorter than me, like most Indonesians, but is stockier, more muscular and healthy in body than most, despite her yellowed eyes. She also has gruffness to her, as an old woman might have. "Will you be here tomorrow?" Lee Lee asks.

I had not thought that far ahead. I glance at Dad, who is grinning a sadistic smile, the wildness in his eyes entrancing a man who sits just across from him. Dad has him sucked in by some hushed, serious tale. I look back to Lee Lee and say, "Most likely. Will I see you?" She nods, smiling, and turns to skip out of the door. I stand for a moment looking after her.

The bathroom is a brightly coloured, damp, cement stall. There is a small, square, porcelain receptacle in one corner, about two feet wide and two feet tall. It is filled with still water and in it floats a red plastic scoop. Next to the water tub are two porcelain footpads on the floor with a hole in between. The napkin Lee Lee gave me, I realize now, is a treasure. I pull it from my hair to use.

The next afternoon, Lee Lee is at the restaurant waiting. She grabs my hand and takes me before I enter, towards the beach where there are women selling fruits, veggies, and goods under brightly coloured shade cloths. I watch three girls jumping rope. I want to join them but know that I am too old and they are not like me. They seem too good and pure, and I have never jumped rope like that before. A group of small children who have been swimming swarm us, laughing and giggling. This is what these travels should be about, I think, smiling with my entire being, at my new friend and the community we are visiting.

Lee Lee and I return to the bar later that evening. I stand to go to the bathroom, feeling the napkins Lee Lee has tied in my hair. When I come back to the table, Lee Lee is gone. Dad's buddy is also gone, and Dad is ready to leave. "Where is your German friend?" I ask him. "He had an appointment with your new friend Lee Lee, in his hotel room." Dad smirks. There is a pounding in my head. I close my eyes and do not know if I can continue to stand.

April 4, 1995—Journal Entry

I continue on to the hotel to read while Dad, Collin, and Bob are at the bar. I now know everyone sees how Dad is, and I don't have to be that way. There is a couple named Dorothy and Retina, whom I meet in the lobby because they are so interested in my bag of books. When I meet them at the bar for dinner, they say that they can help me teach school here if I want, which feels like a dream come true. I also see Lee Lee. She is with the older German man who is working as an engineer here.

She really likes me because I am also a young woman. Later she takes me to a bar called Kareba, where there is a band. We sit and smoke our clove cigarettes and talk some. She knows a bit of English. She is a "working girl," she tells me. I meet some of her friends. I ask if she likes what she does. "Yes yes!" she smiles. "I get good dinner and good hotel." I ask her how much she makes and if it is good business. She says, five bucks a time. Ten thousand rupiahs. Yes, good business. She is spunky. Pretty. I am fascinated to be her friend and I can't help but wonder what it is like, what she does. I know it is taboo and dangerous and sick that these men want this, but she is happy. So are her friends. But they will not always be young, or have nice clients. She does not like to gossip and talk about this.

Lee Lee is proud and seems proud to take me out. She walks with confidence. Her head is back and her shoulders sway. "Two sexy girls," she says as she takes my hand and nearly runs through the crowds on the street. I wonder how one gets this confidence. "I need to work," she tells me. "One hour." We meet the German man in the lobby of a hotel and I reluctantly leave her. Her eyes reassure me. I walk out to the dock to wait near the boats and the ocean and I sit at the end with my legs dangling down. A local guy comes by and sits next to me. He is smooth. He recognizes me from Kareba. "I am in the band! Kareba! I see you!" He is so excited. We have a very nice conversation. He teaches me how to count to five and some other things in Indonesian. Wonderful this innocence under the swirling pink clouds of sunset and dancing, pink flickering waves.

Today is my workday. I go out to the boat to get certain things for Dad and I shop for food, batteries, and other supplies. Funny to think that less than three weeks ago I was in the United States, where the smells and sounds seem so tame. Collin leaves for Australia and I do not get to say goodbye because we are working on the boat. When I finish I take a shower and meet Dad and Bob at the Samarang. Lee Lee and her friend are there and another local crew. Lee Lee has brought two working-girl friends, Emmy and Lily. Lily likes Bob. My dad likes Emmy.

Thank God Dad's morals overcome him even in his drunken state. They have a long, flirty conversation, which Lily skillfully blocks me from. Dad ends up going home on his own and Lily and Emmy can both see that I am being protective of them. Lee Lee and I go to Kareba with her German friend. We dance and laugh and meet friends. We have multicoloured drinks in layers. Some have flames on top. Bob and Lily join us with smiles. My mood changes seeing them and I want to leave, so Lee Lee invites me to stay with her. And the people in the bar won't let me leave. They want me to get up on stage and sing with the band. Ha! I wish I could, but they have no idea of my fear, which suddenly seems so silly.

Lee Lee and her friend and I take a taxi to another local bar, where she sings and we dance merengue. Her German friend looks at her sadly. He tells me she is a survivor and now we are on her own turf. She is a princess here and we dance with all the men and we are protected. He explains the relationship he has with Lee Lee: "Once I arrived I was hounded by whores. When I rejected them they started to send me boys. So I decided to take Lee Lee on as protection. And as an escort." Lee Lee said she was offended when he didn't touch her, and when they got in the bar she got an attitude and wouldn't listen to him anymore. "Now I have to take her to the hotel so she will listen to me."

When we leave they are arguing. We go to the Losari Beach Hotel and this is where my confusion begins. Lee Lee and the German disappear. I wait in the lobby forever. I decide to leave a message for Lee Lee to meet me at the Makassar Golden if she would like. I try to explain the message and also write it down at the front desk. It says, "to Lee Lee, Message from Becky. I am waiting for you in the lobby." Bob and Lily show up and check in. Gross, I think, and leave.

Lee Lee finally runs out behind me, laughing. She explains that the front desk thought I meant to send a massage to her room with the German. They sent another working girl, and he got very angry, so she ran. Lee Lee grabs my hand and pulls me running down the streets through the crowd and food stands until the pavement ends and the lights no longer are there and there are more dogs than people in the streets. There are a few shacks around.

She pulls me into an opening of corrugated metal and we see a labyrinth tunnel path that we have to duck down to follow. I would be lost without her, all of these turns. We finally stop at a wooden board that she knocks on. This is where her brother is. He's lounging on a metal-framed bed with no mattress and that is too small for him. There is a mat on the floor. The three of us stay up and talk.

She takes me to squat on this thing to pee with her before we go to bed. Chickens run behind us. She laughs saying, "It is not the Hotel Makassar Golden!" She washes my feet then we go back to the room. Her brother sleeps on the floor and we sleep on the carpet and a folded blanket. It must be three a.m. before we go to sleep. I sleep well for three hours then we get out to get me back. There are families eating and laughing as we leave the labyrinth. More of her family is here and they are just as smiley as she is. A little one-year-old boy holds my hand through part of the path out.

chapter forty-five

ujung pandang, makassar, indonesia

May 5, 1995—Journal Entry
I go straight to the boat to get the water and gas bins and fill them. Bob meets me. We're both feeling sick. After work we go in a car up to Toraja. It is beautiful and takes all day and I get sick on the way up. There are monkeys running around. The mountains are amazing. The rice fields are so green. Lee Lee gave me a tape of music to listen to and a red shirt. I gave her my favorite dress. We drive to a small cliff-crypt site. There are skulls on wooden shelves on the rock and images of people. There are wooden shrines with big eyes painted on them to honor the deceased. We cross a river via a hanging bridge. We walk through rice fields and into an area where they are building for a celebration. They're constructing bamboo houses and in the centre there is a platform for sacrificing

cows. There are chicken fights. The cocks with their razors. It is so bloody.

We talk with the men of the houses. One of the men is one hundred years old. Each house has an identical counterpart for rice storage. We find that the celebration is for a death. There are many families there. There is a buffalo head freshly cut next to the blood-soaked field in the centre. They bring the casket down from one of the funny houses. One woman cries and wails. It must be the deceased's wife. The casket is placed on a bamboo grid stretcher, which is used to hoist it up and carry it to the rock-cliff graves. The preacher begins. The singing is endless.

The drive down goes more quickly. We stop at an animal market. There are the beautiful, sacred buffalo that are only used for sacrifice and not work. They stand and look on with their big brown eyes as we hand-feed them tender green grass. The pigs are not treated so well. Their legs all tied together and bodies tied down. There is a whole pavilion of them lined up and tied to the floor. The rest of the drive I am mesmerized by the bamboo forests. The rice fields so green and the still waters reflect the mountains, houses, and hills. Even the people working. The men and women in sarongs, picking the rice and thrashing it to get the pods. It is impoverished here—by American standards. All of the houses simple and basic. Such happy, calm faces on the old people. Happy children.

Back at the hotel Lee Lee comes to get me, but I don't feel like going out. She says that because of the argument about the massage her friend did not pay her, so she needs to go out and make twenty dollars for rent. I am sort of pensive and sad, for her, for me. I want us both to have a safe home and someone to love us. A purpose. She cannot continue to work like this. I cannot just hop around and move from place to place like this. Jumping on all of Dad's sails. It disturbs me.

Lee Lee comes back and we go to a bar called Hawaii. All locals there. People start giving her crap about being a lesbian because they think I am her client. Her friend hits on me and gives me her number. Great. We leave and go to the place we went the first night. It is very different this night. There are lots of small tables and karaoke this time. Not so united and very crowded. We sit with two guys because they are the only seats. One of them looks like a slimeball. Greasy pompadour guy. The other is nice. They invite us out. As we leave someone grabs my arm very hard. I am sort of alarmed and jerk away, but Lee Lee gets all over him and he immediately lets go.

We get into a car and drive to some seedy place where the floor is half dirt and half cement. It is crowded and dark with card tables. It almost goes silent when we walk in. I feel like a light bulb in the dark bar. Then the roars of people elevate again and I feel a bit more comfortable. The nice guy tells Lee Lee he can sit and stare at me all night. "Just to look at her beautiful face." He goes on and Lee Lee interprets for me. Finally he asks if he can kiss me and I say no. The rest of the night is a bit awkward, lots of looking down at the ground. Then they ask me where I stay and want me to pay for everything. We have to leave. This is the last I see of Lee Lee.

~~~~~~~~~~

Dhu al-Hijjah is celebrated, the month of the pilgrimage, or hajj, and we are invited. The food is mouthwatering. So many spices and textures, sweets, sours. There are millions of little kids on the streets running through the parades and food carts. As I take photos they come alive dancing and singing and playing, pushing to be in the photos. A young man comes near me to watch. Beautiful, quiet, watching eyes. Confident smile under an odd hat. I am in love for a moment. I hope the photo turns out.

May 12, 1995—Journal Entry

We check out and bring all our things to the boat. Our neighbor from Australia is anchored on his yacht *Golden Hawk* and invites us aboard. It is an Indonesian wooden boat that is 116 years old. He invites us aboard for beers and bangers, sausage on white toast. His ship has tree trunks for masts, old canvas sails. Huge lines. The inside is enormous. There are three forward cabins for the crew. A large main cabin with a bedroom, a double bed, and bath and shower. Big galley and living space. Behind the engine room another captain's chambers. Huge also. His crew all Indonesian—his wife and kid and a bunch of others. One of the crew is beautiful. Long dark hair and skinny, graceful body. Fourteen years old. His eyes are golden yellow with long eyelashes that form like teardrops under his eyes. The captain tells us a story of the "boogies," the old-time pirates who build mobile houses on the reefs in the ocean.

The next morning we depart from Makassar bay towards Sumatra and I take a compass reading: there is no error. Here magnetic north is one and the same as true north. Maybe that is why I feel less tension, more clarity. I do not feel the fear and loneliness that seem to always swell in some degree inside my heart.

A compass does not precisely measure true north on the chart. The magnetic pull of the Earth creates a deviation, which must be mathematically corrected. I had learned the equation for this margin of error, called declination, on the boat when I was small. It is a practical mathematical application, I realize, like counting money or converting funds from one currency to the next, that is necessary for me to know in our travels. Necessary for survival. With the compass reading, the deviation changes from place to place, and from year to year. For example, in Darwin, Australia, in February of 2012, one must add three degrees fifteen minutes east to the compass, or magnetic bearing, to get the true bearing. In Darwin, if the compass points to five degrees, the true bearing is eight degrees fifteen minutes east. This changes by negative 0.035 degrees per year. In Sumatra, in the Indonesian islands, the compass reads nearly exactly as the bearing is.

chapter forty-six

sail to sumatra

~~~~~~~~~~~~~~~

May 25, 1995—Journal Entry
I am in the middle of the Java Sea. It is the fourth day out.
Only puked three times so far, though I have a terrible
cold and fever. It is not as hot today and there is a bit of a
breeze. The first two days we had to motor—so hot, still,
and muggy. Dolphins swim with us in the middle of the
night and the moon is waxing, so the nights are bright. I
can hang out below more often without getting sick. Life
is so different without Lucas on the boat. Almost boring
at times. Thank God for Tolstoy.

I do ballet to keep me limber. But when I throw up,
I cannot move or eat and have a constant hollow in my
stomach. Today I keep couscous down. And I decide
to not take antimalarial medicine, which may be a mistake—but I don't know what will make me more sick, the
medicine, the malaria, or just being on the boat. There
are no fish so far. Lots of ships and fishing boats. The
water is quite dirty. I miss Mom and my sisters. I miss

my job at the museum—so magical studying with those masterpieces in the basement.

Lucas—I am happy that I love him. The illusions are not so strong, now I have a clear perception of him. I fear getting hurt by him. It is hard for me with all of this moving. I will not get close to anyone who will hurt me. I am with people that I know cannot hurt me. Bob is bringing me more in touch with feelings just by navigating being in this small space with him and Dad. None of us has talked much since day two. He annoyed me at first because he was telling me things like an adult would. I hate that. He is honest. He works hard. Dad and I trade off shifts, but Bob does his whole entire shift.

June 1, 1995—Journal Entry

When I wake it is four thirty a.m. and the moon is still full. When the sun rises it is like a film. Forty-five minutes of pure enthralling beauty. The colors creep into the dark sky and blend, lightening the dark, reflecting brilliance on the clouds. The sail has been beautiful. This is our sixth day. And I wait to figure out how many days we have left. Between four and six. I feel great and healthy. I can cook and hang out downstairs without throwing up. I love the cool evenings and mornings. At night I bask in the moonlight on the front deck. In the day I read *Anna Karenina*. It is a bit hot in the day, the sun a bit heavy. I am excited for life. To have confidence. We have 240 miles of 780 left. Clarity. Clarity.

I am excited to study and travel. I pray to get into Stanford for grad school, but it will be hard. My grades are good, some B pluses. I feel ready. I do well on my tests. I have good references and work. It is just my fear of speaking, coupled with my argumentative writing. Today Dad and I listen to the BBC. Lord Tennyson's poem "The

Lady of Shalott" is recited. Then we talk about Kipling, which leads Dad to tell a story about a man in Darwin who fought in the Malaysian war and traveled the world. At seventy-six he beat up three cops for arresting him as a drunk and got off because the judge did not believe it was plausible, and at court the guy recites Kipling. After Tolstoy I read Kipling.

Reading, amidst these sails, has encouraged me to want to lead a pure life and become a lady somehow. I want to learn about religion, Christianity and Islam and Buddhism. Understand all these cultures we visit and the ceremonies and customs and questions they have.

So thankful for the shows of sunset and sunrise that keep me entertained. As the moon rises there are electrical storms and an odd orange glow in the sky—an oil rig burning oil.

There are awkward moments of tense silence between Bob and me. Subtle but there. I avoid his eyes. He put me off a bit in the beginning with his constant lectures as if he could transpose wisdom to me. How I am so young and inexperienced, telling me about money and marriage and fidelity. As if he were married or had money or didn't go off with a hooker. Then showing me how to plot a course while drunk and incomprehensible. He puts his arm around me, his hand on my waist. That blew it and I've kept good distance on this thirty-foot little world.

The heat is sweltering. Dad bought one small fan for down below, connected to his bunk of course. To create some shade, I hang a sheet outside, but the sun is still nasty. It is bearable though. And I can keep my food down, replenish myself with water without puking and even smoke cigarettes. Our meals are beans, canned soup, and tuna, and I make sure to get some canned fruit and corn in there. We have one meal a day plus snacks, not bad. I feel like if I started working out right now, I would keep losing weight, on that downside of normal. This boat could be set up nicely, even with refrigeration. The food could be excellent if Dad allowed me to set it up. But he likes his hell. I understand his mindset is for survival purposes, prepared at any time, but it makes it kind of a hell. Yes, he likes it. Maybe a punishment he feels he deserves.

Dad and I are generally getting on well. He still occasionally orders me around and gets pissed. Still tells me where I can and cannot be, which amuses me. We are floating on a thirty-foot thing with a cabin the size of a pea. When he does this my anger flares up, but I cannot say much. After a while even small comments set me off, like last night on my shift I was doing everything wrong.

Dad does not have enough respect for me to not take me into every bar in the world and show me hookers, his dirty old men and their drunkenness. His sickening drunkenness. Now that I have perspective, I am angry with some of his base views of life. He is well-read and contemplates God, but everything and everyone around us seems to be so rough and dirty. It does not have to be this way. He tells me a dream which brings about pity for him. He dreamt that Freda told him to leave so he went to the bars in Carbondale for solace, but everyone looked down at him. Did not take him in. It made me think how suffocated, psychologically, he actually lets himself get. And how sloppy. And how he gets to talking with such passion and gesticulation. As the spirit demons possess him, his face gets tense and his eyes glow like torches of the hottest flame. And he does not consider or pay attention to others. This is his trip.

But it is hard for me. I so want to learn how to be a lady. I wish to have manners and social graces and be somewhat repellent to dark situations. But this adversity is all I know, where I feel most comfortable. So I hang out with shady people and drink on my own accord and it makes me sad. I am selling myself short.

I have the ability to be nice. A nice girl. And I know it is a large part of me. But then there is that clanking when the gears shift from first to fifth without knowing how to go in between. A dark abysmal crack I want to learn how to bridge. I work so hard to learn, so that I cannot so easily slip to full speed.

I think about getting help, but think I really just need to change my surroundings. When I do that I am fine. So much has to do with self-confidence. The only way I can do that is believe that I am a creature of God or spirit and therefore I must do good, be good. Respect myself and have confidence in myself as a facet of God. But something about religion puts me off. I love that in all these countries and societies religion can bring community and custom, but it also destroys the same. And it tries to explain everything. Humans cannot do that. It puts people at odds with each other. The institution of church scares me and seems hypocritical. But there is a god energy and good in all, and that is what every religion basically narrows down to if felt with love. So I just read *Anna Karenina* and the passage of Levin addresses exactly my ponderings.

Why not another religion? Because I am born in America? But I have spent so much time with these Muslims, Buddhists, Hindus, Jews, and those who do not practice. I am raised in a Christian society (but I did not know that for so long). And why do I have such problems with self-esteem and why do I question religion? Why have I not committed to God? Is it a reflection of my commitment to myself?

I think also about Lucas and love. I respect him so much because he has a solidity to him. He has a serenity, a sturdiness in his manner and eye that enchants me. He moves from place to place and people to people and is accepted, as himself. But then when I think about him asking to marry me, I get angry. Is it only because he needs his citizenship? I believe he cares for me and loves me, but he does not respect me. Though still I feel safe with him and comfortable.

chapter forty-seven

jakarta

〜〜〜

Jakarta—End of Journey

The boat moves slowly through the water in the harbor of Jakarta, maybe because it is so dirty and full of garbage and takes on a sludge-like quality, or maybe because we do not really want to make landing there. This port marks an ending point in our journey. The boat will be dry-docked, wrapped, and put onto a container to Seattle. It is the intended end of the journey, but something about it seems abrupt and sullied.

Dad stands in the cockpit, holding the tiller with one hand, his other hand on his hip. He is bent slightly over at the waist, hunched at the shoulders, and his lower lip juts out in the pursing of his frown. The lines on his forehead are deepened in the many small folds of his furrowed brow. I sit on the bowsprit, but my knees are drawn in tight to my belly, secured by arms clenched around my knees. My toes do not dangle freely in the water like they usually do on such occasions.

I can only see one scraggly palm tree on a litter-strewn beach next to the industrial dock where we are headed to check in with immigration. We can see the Indonesian flag drooping on a flagpole in the stagnant heat, and below are curls of barbed wire atop a high, chain-link fence. Behind the fence is a square, concrete building, guarded by men in full military uniform, and weapons of some sort. I feel nauseous. The smell of fish and oil are strong and the heat seeps into my pores. I feel layers of dirt and exhaust accumulate the closer we get. The small fishing vessels part as we arrive. The men in them look at *Cattle Creek*, and her crew, with serious, intent stares. No one smiles or waves, from either side.

As we approach the dock, Dad props himself up to wave and gives gestures of peace and respect, only to be welcomed by yelling and an ever-growing crowd of military personnel. Impatient jabs in our direction with weapons. I secure the buoys on the port side of the boat as we slowly ease up to the dock. I ready the dock line, secure it to the bow, then jump to the dock to tie it off to a cleat. The dock feels hard and unforgiving under my sea legs. I run along the solid, hot dock to the stern of the boat to catch the line from Dad as he kills the engine and begins his work to appease the officials. I secure the boat, not knowing whether to follow Dad towards the customs building, or to stay on the boat and watch our gear, alone. The point of a machine gun answers my question. I quickly stow the binoculars, and whatever other valuables I see, lock the hatch of the boat, and run off to gain on Dad and his new entourage. Bob disappears, eager to be on land.

The customs building has two small windows and no air conditioning. There are ropes set up in a maze to direct people to the long customs counter at the far end of the room. There are only two other men in line, and they look like fishermen. The man behind the desk yells at the fisherman whose turn it is, then as he pushes his documents towards him, shaking his head and gesturing for the fisherman to leave. He does, with his head bowed. Dad looks at me with wide eyes and raised eyebrows; I know he is suppressing a whistle to indicate the challenge we are about to face, but he holds it back. I give him a half smile and take a seat at the back of the room. Maybe this will go fast, I think as I see Dad standing in first position in the maze. The official behind the desk speaks quietly but sternly with the man who is now trying to accomplish something.

Sweat is dripping off my forehead. I feel it travel from my hairline, over my forehead, pause in my eyebrow, then cascade down my face, stinging my eye and leaving a taste of salt in the corner of my mouth. I am thirsty. My tongue is heavy and my spit is thick and foamy. An official is staring at me. I shift away in my chair slightly and hunch over. How can he stand here in full dark uniform, day in, day out? No wonder they do not smile.

Dad is losing his cool. He wavers back and forth on his feet, switching his weight from one leg to the other. A fly hovers near his shoulder and neck, occasionally landing. Dad swats at it violently, as if it is a bad thought. I know he is feeling queasy standing on solid ground, wanting the gentle rock of the ocean that has been pulled from under him like a rug. I know he wants a beer. I see the spirit in his face droop, and his struggle to keep a respectful countenance about him.

The clock on the wall ticks loudly, and the minutes crawl by, adding up. We have been there an hour and twenty minutes now, and the official is still lecturing the man at the counter. Finally, the sound of the stamp. Officials love stamps. This man has a black leather case for his, and he pulls it out reverently. It is a large stamp, with a long, wide shaft and an oversized ball to hold and press down to make the mark. The man slowly places his palm on the ball, wrapping his fingers around it one by one, then forcefully slams the apparatus down. I wince. Three times in a row on three different papers in front of him, *chchclunk, chchclunk, chchclunk*. The sound seems deafening after all the silence. Everyone's posture straightens, except the man who has his papers stamped, who silently gathers them and leaves. The official lifts his gaze to Dad, cracks his knuckles, and grins widely.

When I see that Dad may be nearly finished, I have to go outside. The air pours heavily into my lungs. I see a pay phone and call Lucas. He has found a home. Not a shack or container, but a house. With his girlfriend. I have finished college. But I lost my love. It must be better this way, but my heart hurts.

<hr />

In the morning I go with Dad to the embassy. Dad meets a marine there who invites us to the marine club. I am pissed to have to go to another bar, but once we get there my attitude changes.

"Officer Riley." The marine stretches his hand out from his starched, fatigue-patterned sleeve, a stern look on his face. "Show me to the bar," Dad says as he grabs his hand and firmly shakes it. The officer smiles. "Yes, sir. Follow me." I know it is going be an even longer, more arduous day for me, though the celebration is about to begin for Dad. I look back towards the boat, hoping for a bag of clothes and books, my journal, but I just follow Officer Riley. His head is shaved, and he is short and stocky. He has handsome, dark eyes and moves with a quickness and efficiency appropriate for military personnel.

We make it out of the customs compound and walk behind the building, so we cannot see the water. I scamper up to Dad. "Dad, can I get some clothes and maybe rinse off?" I quietly beg him. He puts his hand on my head and ruffles my hair. "Officer," he calls. Officer Riley turns around. "Any chance we can grab a change of clothes from the boat and clean up a bit?"

"Call me Riley. Yes. Let's go." We come to the end of the building and head back towards the boat. I run ahead and grab some soap, my bag with Tolstoy and my journal, and a change of clothes. We are in a Muslim area, and around marines and fishermen in a foreign place, so I throw in a long-sleeved cotton shirt and a long skirt. My feet need to be covered as well. Dad grabs his Levi jeans, a "nice" shirt, which means it has a collar, and a razor he throws in his duffel bag. I learn to be quick, or else I would "miss the boat," so to speak.

Riley is surprised at our speed. "You military or something?" he jokes, then checks himself, regaining composure. We are brought to the Port Marine Bar, which has a nice air-conditioned entryway that reminds me of a living room that might come out of the 1950s. It is the cool I feel most, as I look around at the dimly lit room. There is a dark carpet under a somewhat ornate, wooden-framed couch and chairs set in dark red velour. Through a set of glass doors I can see the bar. A row of stools in the smoky haze lead to the huge picture window beyond, which looks out to the busy industrial bay.

Riley shows me to a door and opens it for me. It is a ladies' powder room, with a small stool in front of a vanity. I feel like I am walking into a museum set. Off to the side is another door that holds a proper toilet; there is even toilet paper. I lock the door behind me, and slink my back down the door to sit on the floor. I feel as if I have been transported to a safe place that is not this loud, dirty, hot city, where I am not just at the whims of Dad and whatever the next moment has in store for me. I have no idea that this feeling couldn't be further from the truth.

I take a sort of sponge bath, brush my hair and teeth, and change from my grimy boat clothes. I finally emerge from the powder room clean and refreshed. I see Dad and Riley huddled at the bar on their stools. I walk over to the fragile-looking couch. I sit, pulling *Anna Karenina* from my bag, and become immersed.

Dad and Riley finish an innumerable number of beer bottles. Arms, hands, and voices rise higher into the air as I finally get to the end of the book. I set the book to rest on my lap, my butt is asleep, and I wonder what to do. Go back to the boat on my own in the dark, and risk being harassed by the unknown men who lurk on industrial docks after dark? That would be stupid. I cannot read anymore, and I do not want to sit at the bar, drink a Coke, and have my head throb with the familiar rotten beer, stale smoke smell, and pounding, nonsensical noise that comes from men at bars. I know Dad will be in the mood to hug me and praise me and turn all eyes to me and spew his drunken pride on me. It makes me feel wrong or bad when he does that. Something about it is not right. It is that ever-encrusted layering of insecurity, confusion, and uncertainty around, and clutching at, my heart.

I go into the bar, pull up a stool beside Riley, and order a drink. Something I have never done before with him on my own. I engage with the men he is talking to there, including Riley, Ed, and some others. They ask me, as if I am a human too, about what I am doing and I tell them about Dorothy and Retina, who say they will help me become a teacher here. I tell them about sailing and reading. And I tell them all this in front of Dad, and he is surprised and curious. And I feel interesting. They invite us to go out, and Dad has that hunched over the bar, Jack Nicholson look, and I know he couldn't go out even if he wanted to. So I look at him, and them, and then I smile and say, "Yes, I'd love to."

My journal entry from that night:

I somehow stand, walk into the bar, do not sit next to Dad, but on the other side of Riley, and I order a beer. Dad looks at me and raises his eyebrows in surprise, and warning. It makes me look down into my beer, clasp it tightly with both hands. After we talk a bit, Riley excuses himself.

I begin to feel the light freedom that emerges from stepping over the threshold of choosing to join in on the drinking. This feels exposed, but I know my other choices entail subjecting myself to danger, or to ultimate anger towards Dad for neglecting my needs. I am choosing to take part. I can make my own decisions for myself, probably better than Dad can. I begin to speak with some of the other bar patrons, who are very courteous, and also very obviously barely containing themselves that they are able to talk to a young blond American girl. As I enjoy myself more, Dad becomes more quiet. His shoulders hunch heavily over the bar, and his eyes look sadly over at me, under a heavy brow, that bobs ever so slightly, with his booze-soaked state.

Riley returns, wearing jeans and a button-down shirt. He has shaved and I notice that he smells like soap. We have another beer. He is from Portland, Oregon. He has been stationed in Jakarta for just over a year. "What do you do here, when you are not on duty?" I ask.

"Work all day, so mostly go out at night. It is fun to meet up with expats and travelers, and show them around, or have them take us somewhere new," Riley responds, looking me squarely in the face, with an earnest expression, as if he is still on duty.

"Do you have a girlfriend?" I do not know what else to ask, and feel stupid as soon as it comes out. I see I have disarmed him.

A shy smile creeps over his face. A pause before he speaks. "There are a lot of hookers here, Becky. We call them ayam." He looks down, almost shamefully, then looks at me again flat in the eyes and does not look away. I am surprised by his answer. Upfront. Matter of fact. Respectful. This is my choice to be here and he knows it is something I do not normally do. He lays the cards on the table.

I sigh, relax my shoulders, and smile. "I know. I just met this girl. I thought she would be my friend, and she is a hooker." I tell him about Lee Lee. Riley looks at me. I know Dad told him about me, that I had seen it all but did not take part. I have learned to overlook, almost as if I am blind to certain things, obscuring reality, filtering it. But tonight is different. I have had enough of Dad just doing what he always wants without regard to my needs. I always feel like a girl who needs a shower, and a bathroom. I want to have good food when I am hungry, not canned food or peanuts that are provided in the bars. I want to see the markets and meet friends. I want to go to the countryside and meet decent families, see farms, mountains, statues, and gardens. I do not want to see people have sex. To see and hear obscenities in bars. To always be fixing the mess of what is left behind, never to be able to do anything for myself in the first place.

~~~~~~~

I hear Riley talking to me but cannot stop my head from thinking: Dad has been in charge. If we are not with the wild, obscure characters that give him beer or weed or sex, or whatever else he finds through them, we do not associate with them. Now, tonight, I am doing something on my own. I see him there at the bar and feel so angry at him. "Let's go out," I finally hear. Yes, I think. Yes. "I'd love to. YES, I'd love to," I say to Riley and stand. I have to place my hand on the stool to steady myself.

"Wait. Are you sure? It is getting late," I say. I instinctively look for Dad, who is nowhere to be seen. He has left me here, alone. Riley sees the terror in my eyes and hesitantly puts a comforting hand on my shoulder. "He told me to watch you like a hawk. You are in good care." I look at Riley with what feels like piercing, animal, intuiting eyes. The gaze causes him to shift slightly back. I decide I will trust him.

Riley holds out his hand to guide me out of the bar, out of the cozy little 1950s living room, into the sultry black night that envelops us.

Riley hails a rickshaw for us, and offers me his hand to climb in. I pause. Normally, I would shun any such gesture, taught that accepting help from another meant indebtedness to them. But, my rebellion to Dad surges. And I want to be a lady. I see my hand reach out to accept his. He simply helps me step into the cart. I do not owe him anything. In fact, as I look at him, I realize that he has no idea that these thoughts are even in my head. I feel a sense of triumph. I feel womanly, a fantasy of myself. I feel respected and proud. Then all at once, as we head towards the interior of the city and the noises escalate, the proliferation of neon lights blurs my eyesight. I shrink back down into myself, vulnerable and afraid.

We go to Top Gun, which is a velvet-carpeted, round-tabled, cigar-darkened joint that may have been classy in the 1940s. Riley watches my reactions. He pulls out a cushioned armchair for me, and asks what I would like to drink. "Bintang, right? It is the local beer?" I reply.

Riley looks at me with a furrowed brow, then his confusion lifts and he responds, "Would you like to try a glass of wine, or maybe a drink?"

I realize that I just assumed I'd get what Dad drank, and I feel stupid, and know that Riley knows. "Please choose for me." I look at him, knowing he sees my vulnerability.

When he leaves I take a deep breath and settle into my chair. I look around and see men in suits, smoking cigars, tucked into the corners speaking with one another. An American man in a dressy marine uniform, having dinner with a dainty Asian woman. His face is pale, soft, and youthful. It barely looks like he shaves. I think of Lucas and the thick stubble on his tanned, angular face. I close my eyes and think of him. I am surprised to find, in my thoughts, him kissing me. I become aware of a stir in my lower abdomen, and feel a heated expansion pressing slightly against the cushion below me, between my sit bones. My eyes fly open when I hear the tinkling of ice on glass, as Riley sets the drink in front of me. "Are you okay?" he asks, looking concerned.

"Tell me about the boat. Your travels." I take a drink of something lightly sweet and carbonated, and feel a warm flush in my cheeks and belly just after I swallow.

Somehow, immersed in our conversation, we leave and walk outside to another location. Riley grabs my hand and pulls me into the misty rain to a diner sort of place. It does not completely dawn on me that this happens until I stop talking, and we stop in a flood of light on the sidewalk in front of large glass windows. Behind the glass are striking women, swaying narrow hips, reaching long slender arms towards the air, interlacing meandering forearms, wrists, and fingers, slowly rolling heads back to expose smooth, precious necks and graceful, arched jaw-lines upholding pouting lush and open lips. I just stare. Riley looks at me curiously, and softly, he tilts his head and watches them too, in a different way. "They are beautiful," I say.

"They are," Riley whispers.

Inside, behind the women on display, light-colored wooden booths are sectioned off by walls of white with neon lights constructed in tubes within them. They blink in a sequence traveling up, around, then down, up, around, then down. Young people swarm, talk, smile, drink. There are cute little tank tops and short, silky skirts. Exotic eyes flirt under teal and golden eyeliner and fashionable bangs. I put my hand to my chest, feeling very unsexy in the conservative clothes I have chosen to hide myself in. Riley stands to grab two drinks from a tray that circulates, and sits next to me. We both quietly watch.

"Riley!" a loud man slaps his shoulder, then swirls around to sit across from us in the booth, grabbing Riley's hands, smiling warm and close, over the table. He reaches over, taking my hand in both of his, staring at me intently in the eyes with a devious smirk. "Don. Officer Don Stook. What is this lovely young thing's name, Riley?" Still looking me in the eyes. His hands are clammy, puffy, and soft.

Riley methodically separates Don's hands from mine. "This young lady is Becky. She and her dad sailed in today. I'm showing her around."

"I bet you are," Don says, and then squeezes his arm around a small, pretty girl next to him on the bench. His fingers crawl down under her tank top, pull at the top of her bra. The girl notices my gaze at her; eyes barely visible under lowered bangs, she looks woozy and distant. Behind the girl, beautiful girls in small outfits flit around, laugh. They flirt. Looking out under lashes, sipping from bright-colored straws. I take a drink of what is in front of me, feeling a lightness and buzzing from the alcohol warming my blood. *Who are these girls? Are they hookers?* I think. "Who are these girls?" I hear myself blurt to Riley and Don. The table becomes quiet, they all look at me.

"She speaks," smiles Don as he stands to leave, with his girl attached to his side.

I ask Riley, "Are they all hookers too? Is she a hooker?" I whisper about the girl with Don, who is not paying attention to anything. "Some are, some not. Some only for tonight."

"Do they like it?"

"They make money. In places like this, they are usually treated well."

"They look so young."

"Sexually curious. Weren't you then? Or . . . aren't you?"

"Then? Now? I guess so . . ." I squeeze my legs together.

Don and his lady had gotten up to move around the crowd, to flirt and move and feel bodies pass close to them. I feel myself sinking in towards Riley's shoulder, and feel his warmth. I look at him looking at the scene. "Do they really like this?" I ask again, looking back to the girls dancing in the window, knowing how uncomfortable and sick I would feel if I were them.

"They look happy. And no one is twisting the arms of these particular girls. Maybe it is all a sham. But, it is a beautiful sham. And a natural one," he says. "They do seem happy," I say. I settle into him and we watch.

Some who know him already come in giggling and cuddle in next to us to take us to the next place. It is a disco, with balconies of obviously unsafe architecture crowded with bands mimicking Michael Jackson and others. There is an old, classic theatre seating area where waitresses in tiny black leotards carry platters high above their heads and bring glow-in-the-dark drinks. Up the stairs, a woman fingers "come" to Riley and he is lured to a chair where she sways her tiny hips and pelvis and tight, round buttocks lusciously in his lap. The whole time I know I drink at least a few whiskies and try to have a psychological conversation with Riley, the men, the hookers and dancers about why they choose to live this life and what underlying socio-political-economic, intuitive yearning or drive causes this lifestyle . . . seeing so clearly the effect of American soldiers plopped into a culture and given working girls to appease their needs and the ramifications that have snowballed in every society and gender and psyche it has touched.

Don comes back alone, visibly more inebriated. "Next stop, Riley. C'mon man." Riley looks at me questioningly and I nod. The next bar is larger, more extravagant than anything I have ever seen. It reminds me of a stage I may have seen on TV set up for a Madonna performance. Rising pillars moving slowly up and down topped with small girls dancing on their platforms. Lights shoot everywhere in beams in which particles flicker silver and yellow, amidst curling plumes of smoke.

Riley opens his mouth to mimic the jaw-dropped expression on my face, and smiles. Don brings us drinks that are layers of colors, and flaming on top. "Follow me," Riley says to me, seeing that my senses need someplace to recover. We climb a wide, maroon-carpeted staircase that winds around a wall, behind which is another stage slightly more elevated. I try not to burn my face or hair with the drink, walk up the stairs, and watch what is going on all at once.

At the top of the stairs my head swims, but I feel alert and cannot stop staring at everything. We come to a lounge area on a mezzanine overlooking the world below. Deep black couches and lounge chairs tuck back against the dimly lit back wall, and only a few people linger here. Riley offers me a seat, and he sits across from me, smiling, as a woman with a tray of drinks comes by. My eyes travel curiously from the woman's black high heels holding perfect red toenails x-ed with fishnet stockings that crisscross up to a short black-leather minidress. I reach up and grab a glass with the most innocuous-looking thing in it and drain it as I watch another woman in a similar dress behind Riley, trailing her long red nails up his arm, over the back of his shoulders and down the other arm. I sober up, feel something sick and tight in my stomach, and notice, surprised, the clarity of my head.

She looks at me, sensually, then squats at Riley's feet. "Lap dance for you? Or for your lady?" she asks. He smiles at her and shakes his head no. "I am right over here if you change mind," her words drip onto him. I can see him shift in his chair as his eyelids close slowly.

"Do it!" I say, without believing I said it. "You would if I were not here."

He just looks at me, looking tired, almost agitated, and sharply asks, "Do you want to watch?" I hate him now. Hate Dad for letting me leave. Mostly hate myself for thinking I can do this. For thinking I can do anything. My face grows hot and I slump into my chair, distinctly aware of the presence of my vagina. It says yes. Yes? Yes?! What is wrong with me?

"Yes," I reply with eyes open wide, sinking back further into the chair, trying to make myself invisible. I have exposed something black inside of me. It scares me.

Riley drains his drink, sets it down. Beaded drops of water slide down the side of the glass and pool around it on the table. He lifts his hand and nods his head towards the woman, who has been leaning against the wall, watching us. She first looks away, her smile slowly creeping more deeply across her face. She lifts her hips slowly away from the wall, then presses her shoulder blades to the wall to push her body away from it, and towards Riley. Slowly sauntering as if she is bored and has nothing better to do, she nearly walks past him, stepping over his outstretched legs that are crossed at the ankle, then abruptly turns to him mid-step and rips off the lower skirt portion of her dress. Her butt cheeks, small and firm, face me. They are white behind the black crisscross stockings, framed by the dainty line of a G-string that runs along her lower hips, T-ing down and disappearing, emerging thicker as a shadow between her legs, revealed on the other side, swaying, straddled over Riley's upper thighs. Her small, graceful hands drift up the sides of her body and reach back behind her neck to lift her hair up, slowly, on top of her head, as she arches her back, turning to smile at me. I want to disappear. The woman drops her hands down to Riley's shoulders, thrusts her behind back towards me. It sways back and forth like the pendulum in a clock, delayed but ticking off time. Her knees step up onto the chair just outside of Riley's thighs and she presses her chest towards his face.

The lights blur by in streaks through the taxi window. My head has that pounding again.

"Doesn't anyone understand how fucked up this all is? The military outposts, the wars, these women?" I try to explain to Riley in the taxi. I am somehow receptive to his kisses as I verbally investigate what is going on until I realize we are passing the port and pulling up toward high-security barracks, at which point I become quiet.

What has happened in this night, in just a few short hours, has packed in worlds of meaning of culture and sex and youth and corruption and war and military and innocence and passion. And time, and timelessness. I think of the video on the theory of relativity I saw in school in which a bike, a taxi, and a rocket travel at proportionately increasing speeds relative to the speed of light and time slows down for the rocket because it is moving so quickly. I did not understand this idea until just now.

Riley reaches across the seat to place his hand on mine. I close my own hand tight into a fist.

"What are you going to tell your dad?" he asks. "He will get a kick out of all of this."

The taxi slowly passes the military port. I can see the cranes that lift the cargo crates onto ships and I smell the richness of the ocean.

"I don't want to tell him anything. I don't want to see him." I feel my eyelids droop, my head sag against the window.

The barracks are past the port, just beyond the depth of the city. White, blocky structures glowing slightly in the darkness, umbrellas by waving palms. We drive through the guarded entrance gate and I stagger from the cab into a warm, breezy air that smells of rich, tropical flowers. Riley helps me walk. I see my feet move on the wet pavement, as if they are not mine. Then we are in his room. It is small, and neat. A square room with two small windows with bars on them, in the tradition of every residential building I have seen in Indonesia. There is a desk with a bible, a notepad, and a pen. Shoes are set neatly in pairs, polished, by the door. And his bed is smooth—made as I would imagine a military bed to be made. The room smells of sandalwood soap and the gentle breeze that passes around me.

Riley circles his arms around my lower back as I try to splash water onto my face and mouth in the little sink by the door. Then he presses his lips to mine. I feel slack in his arms; I taste the alcohol, feel his cold lips, and I squeeze my thighs together. He is not Lucas. This is not love. Is this what people, the girls in the bars, feel?

I feel his hardness on my hip as he moves me to his bed, where I just want to sleep in black. Want to go away. He is removing his shirt, trying to unbutton mine, kissing my neck as he steps out of his jeans. I curl into a fetal position on the bed, trying to stop spinning. He slides strong hands under the waistline of my skirt and pulls his hips close to mine. His awkward hands try to slide my skirt off as I grasp it hard to my belly. I curl tighter into his bed. He gropes at my clothes and climbs over me and attempts to push his girth, which feels disproportionate and uncomfortable, into me; then he collapses from the alcohol.

I feel cold in my belly. Then darkness everywhere.

Birds chirp deafeningly loud as I open my eyes. My heart is gripped and I am blinded by the pale yellow streams of sunlight coming through the barred windows. I look over at Riley, still passed out, aware of a blurring weight in my head. Quietly, I stand and fix my clothes. I go to the door and flee the room. I skirt the building, squeeze through the security entrance without even looking to see if there is a guard, and run down a small street in the direction of the city until I find, and flag, a rickshaw to take me back to *Cattle Creek*.

Dad is on the dock, rinsing lines and preparing buckets and brushes and Comet soap for cleaning. His chest is sweating and I can smell his familiar, sweet beer man smell.

"How was it?" he asks, looking at the dock, hands on his hips.

I do not know what to say. *How was it?* I repeat the question to myself and hold back tears. I know I am blessed to be back on *Cattle Creek*, safely.

chapter forty-eight

career

~~~~~~~~

July 1, 1995—Journal Entry
We dock at the Ancol Marina, which has a beautifully manicured garden of trees, flowers, and grass around the parking lot, but the rest is odd. One restaurant, very expensive, overlooking mudflats and an ocean reeking of sewage. We decide to wander into town to find a shower. Dad is out of it. He is frustrated that we cannot find a shower, and in his impulsive mood he takes us back to fill the toilet bucket and dumps it over his head. But I find a shower.

The Hotel Horizon is down the dock and has cold white-marble floors. There is a gong that announces our entry and I want to shrink and hide. Dad buys a room for $102 a night. While Dad jumps on a motorcycle with the immigration official and ventures towards the inner-city customs buildings, I meet with the woman who will help organize the shipping of our boat. She is very bright and we enjoy each other's company. We have to get two containers at $4000 apiece for the boat to ship on the Maersk shipping line. I ask her about shipping other goods and learn a lot. She tells me about local crafts and museums and art and writing. The boat should be approved by Wednesday and shipped to Seattle in the next couple of days.

Dad is not back, so I take a bet-jack to the museum she tells me about, The Museum National. Beautiful contemporary Balinese paintings. Patterned. Detailed and intricate. I like the simple drawings. There are carvings of stone artifacts. I buy a blow gun. Dad is at the hotel shit-faced before his meeting at three p.m. for the boat. I leave and find food from a stall and sit in a playground near one of the mashallas, or prayer places. There is an art market I want to see. Bob is ready to leave. Dad's drinking spell is getting to him too. With each day I get more antsy and pissed. Like I am spinning my wheels. The monotony of each day. Dad goes to the bar early afternoon and drinks. By five he is loaded. By seven beyond and by eight or nine goes to bed. Last night he slept in the bar chair. I have PMS.

At least there are other interesting people. Anton is a young guy from South Africa who works out of Hong Kong, and his German partner lives in Singapore. Anton is attractive and I feel awkward around him. Inadequate and insecure and pitiful because of my situation. We also meet an American named Jeff, who is so nice. I have to get out of here. Maybe I can stop in Hong Kong to visit my friend from school, Anis. I will go to more museums. Maybe I can find a play or something to see.

We continue to be busy concerning the boat as well as new businesses Dad has conjured up. I have gotten several things at the art market and bargained well. He wants to incorporate the Balinese-style carvings into the homes he builds. He wants me to figure out how to find and ship carvings and furniture for him. I had already been doing this for textiles for myself, but he is offering to loan me $5000, which is tempting, but I would still be involved with him. My own business is already, in my mind, called Saffron Inc., and will import textiles, art dyes, woodwork, and ceramics. I telephone Anis in Hong Kong and she tells me her mom lives near where we are. I call her mom, Meili, and she picks me up with her husband and Anis's little sister.

Meili takes me to her home, in a gated expat community, for dinner. I walk into a huge marble entry with a winding marble staircase. Opera is drifting in like it is wind. They have five maids. As we are served, she tells me about Indonesian commerce culture and about products and quality. Regions of specialty. The local cultures and the beauty and history of their crafts. It is refreshing to sit in a clean courtyard and have meaningful discussions.

Meili later invites me to meet with her friend who supplies all the regional hotels with local decor. She will also show me furniture the next day. Hand-carved, regional wood. Some exploited and unattainable, some not, which is of concern to me, but I know to keep that to myself now and do something about it later. We drive to different markets to look at silk, wood, ceramics, and other art. We take breaks at cafés to rest and talk. Most importantly, she shows me photos of Anis and all the articles written about her. Anis is interviewed for the high-society magazines of Hong Kong for her community involvement, and who knows what else. I am so proud of her.

~~~~~~~~

Meili takes me to an open-air market and makes me find something to bargain for. I pick a carved voodoo-like figure and call him "Boogie."

"Five pesos," I say.

"Twenty," the man says. "Last one."

I say, "Ten." He gives it to me and for a moment I am proud. Then he goes into the back and replaces it with another one just like it.

"First," Meili says, "don't ever start first. You could have gotten that for three." Okay, lesson learned. I decide to stay in Jakarta and do research on importing furniture, carvings, silk, Balinese doors.

I say goodbye to Dad. I am leaving this sailing life I know. I don't want to in so many ways, but I also know this life will only pull me down. I have to figure out my own path. We are relieved to be parted, and it pains my heart. But love is undeniable, in all its forms.

part IV

.

chapter forty-nine

memory

～～～～～

Dad always warned us that he might die, anytime he went sailing. Charlie and Gregg and Carl could have been shot by pirates, but they were not. Dad knew his risk in the places he went and the ways in which he went there . . . and such is life. You never know.

December 23, 1996—Journal Entry
4:27 a.m. I walk down the hall towards the kitchen and, as hoped, hear rustling upstairs in Dad's room. The genetic and psychological donor of my insomnia. The only one suffering with me, with whom I could share the few magic parts associated with it—the mystic dreams and thoughts of those wee morning hours. Like old times, I whisper his name as I hesitate to climb the steps. "Come on up, Bexter!" Like when I was younger and lived with him, I run up the stairs and jump into the big chair by his bed, cuddling in the worn blanket there. He immediately delves into the dream he was having when he woke up.

I did not know this would be the last time we would be together like this.

I watched the life in his face, wondering why I had never drawn that face. So many others I had drawn, nameless models I spent hours tenderly molding the curve of a high cheekbone, or sadness at the corner of an eye. I would make up stories behind a slight crease in a forehead, a shadow of a breast. But I knew his story. The paths creeping back from the soft skin beside his lower eyelid, marking fifty-five years of laughter and life in the sun. Deep-lined forehead revealing surprise, wonder, endless thought-repeating expressions so familiar to that skin. Indented tracks beside his mouth revealing hints of sadness, and room to accommodate a smile larger than expected.

I want to draw this face, resisting the urge to reach out and touch the strong jawline of my dad. His spirit dances like the wind in his hand gestures, and shines in the cobalt flecks of his eyes. It speaks in the silence of his words. As can a drawing. Done with knowing, done with love. This old soul, full of passion. Adventure. Wise and brimming beyond this body, this time.

chapter fifty

motherhood

~~~~~~~~~

October 20, 2009—Journal Entry

Propped up on pillows I wait. Ingrid, my midwife, snuggles on a beanbag chair in the corner with her books. Her medical kit with supplies: ointment, large absorbent pads, and antiseptic. Was Mom making tea for me? Was she sitting down eating the zucchini bread she had made in case someone got hungry? My husband might be outside. Creating lines in the lawn with too many passes of his rake.

The room is sparsely furnished—a bed and a dresser. I brought in homey things like candles and shells over the past several weeks. There is music of my memories on a homemade CD: Bob Dylan, Bob Marley, Enya.

The skin of my belly stretches before me, like the roundness of the Earth. My mind races to tales I have read. A woman in a cabin lying on a straw mattress with woolen blankets piled under her. The candle flickers. Crunching forward, mouth open in silent scream. Sweat dripping into the corners of her eyes. When she is done, they pack her with a pumice of hay and dung to stop the bleeding. They wonder why the fever begins, and why the blood oozes to green, why she becomes still.

I slow my breath. My mind feels weary behind my eyelids, which try to close and let me rest after so many hours in labour. I think of the river Yangtze long ago. Women gave birth there and then too. Flowing, pastoral, and peaceful. Then rocks. Bashing white water spraying into light. By the river is a hut in which a woman swells. She digs her heels into this big spinning Earth, under the moonlight. She resists. Beads of sweat form on her temples. She breathes deep and guttural. She falls, finally, against the rotation of the Earth, shudders and moans deeply, and her baby sings its first cry.

Mom does not come down. Where is she? I moan. The O in Woman, the wide-open lips singing in chorus, the warm open O: emotion. The WO, the enchantment, the mystery.

Ingrid brings a cool, soothing cloth to my forehead, wiping back strands of soaked hair. I breathe deeply, slowly, in rhythm again.

Two weeks overdue, I see a naturopath recommended by Ingrid. Gaea is six feet tall and proportionally large, not overweight, but grand, like her name. She expertly inserts needles into my lower back, or upper hips, I cannot tell, but it just feels like cold on bone. And something shifts. A fluttering spasm of muscles gathers there then swarms forward. That was yesterday.

Again it comes on. I watch my belly lurch and harden to square corners. It clenches down hard. I wretch. Yellow bile, warm fluid, dripping from my lips. But this time someone puts a cool rag on the corner of my mouth. It may even be my mom, again, after so many years.

I think of all kinds of births. At a farmhouse in the middle of nowhere a man prays and the children run from the field to the porch to the kitchen, yelling and slamming doors. The woman silently curses him for not letting her go to the hospital. "As God would have it," he tells her. She remembers all too clearly and with fear the last one stillborn.

Who else on this Earth is doing this now? The girls in Jakarta? On Thursday Island? If we all moan together, can we stop the spin? I slowly stand to go to the bathroom, but a cannonball grounds me down, not caring about my pelvic bones. Its gravity brings me to my knees. Ingrid guides me down. A shudder slowly travels up the muscles of my spine, like lightning flashing on the ocean. Then it rushes, flows, out, free, flowing with life.

O—is it capable? A deep breath to exhale the breath of all women. A burning, cutting sting, a rush like hot lava. I close my eyes and slump down. My husband catches my hand lightly, bringing it down. I feel the small head. The small body is brought squirming from under me, inside me, up to my breast, erasing it all.

July 18, 2012—Journal Entry

2:09 a.m. Today would be Dad's birthday. I look through my drawings of a model; unnamed, unknown, remembering the way the sun lit the room, the music that played, as if it were today. But there is no spirit in these portraits. His face fades in memory, after all these years. It is gone. Why did I not draw his face, the man I knew with my heart, and loved and sometimes hated, with the cells of my being? So I could show his spirit to my children.

chapter fifty-one

everything

~~~~~~~~~~

After all those years of pretending. Pretending to want to live in a house in town, instead of a cabin in the woods or, really, a boat on the ocean. To achieve, own a business, to succeed, instead of gallivanting around the world like the gypsy that I am born of seed pearl in saline miasma, floating by currents, wind, waves. Constructing a framework around me to be normal and defined. But really just needing to run and sing as it pours down rain.

Coming home on time after one-and-a-half glasses of wine. Trying to mute the colors and melody that burst through my thoughts. The songs that call me to sail into tropical lagoons, climb mountains, sing beautiful and loud in a cathedral, to jump off sand dunes too high. But now I have a girl and a boy. A house in a town. A husband. Responsibility. Society. Building beautiful homes. Teaching art and world culture to little kids. Community. Everything I have always wanted. And I have to pretend that I am not wild, that I am contained. That my thoughts don't waver as they do. I have to watch the other moms to make sure I learn when to say to my children it is too high and to stop climbing. Everything is safer than the boat and I have no idea what I am doing. It would be too dangerous, too wild, to not pretend. And, it would be too perfect to be in love with it all.

chapter fifty-two

sulu sea

~~~~~~

March 14, 2015—Journal Entry
But I want to go back to the Sulu Sea. To the ocean. Gales whistling through halyards, small, stubbed, bloody toes running on lurching decks tripping over metal cleats.

~~~~~~

I write that I want to be in a boat on the Sulu Sea, while in this chilly mountain cabin I wear a knit hat snuggled over ears, cold dry hands toiling over keyboard from half-fingered mittens, warm breath turning to spirit of the cold air in the little living room. Fogged windows reaching with crystals blur a herd of elk that roam the field outside. Steam rises from their bodies. They live . . . live . . . outside. Breathe a breath of mist. I want to live outside. Eyes stinging with salt water, sun-warmed skin, spices in a marketplace, knowing eyes.

And I tell him I have to leave. I told him first in my own mind. What once seemed such possibility, all those things I thought I should do, this home and this marriage, the things so different from what I had lived. What school and society made me feel was opportunity, now that I have done them, feel confining. And I know in my heart, from the ocean, from the boat, from my dad, that when we don't confine ourselves there is no end to possibilities. You need truth, faith, love and virtue, and a bit of moderation to guide you the right way, but you need not be limited. Now I feel everything boxing me in, suffocating me. Every morning, as I hold our smiling children, all I seem to hear from him are his rants of frustrations with politics and everything that is impossible, of people and humanity minimized, places dejected of all their earthly magic. I hear this spew endlessly from dark hanging clouds. Too much of what is wrong, not enough of the magic of possibility. We have babies who turn into little humans. And eventually they soften each of us. But after eight years, I can only remember and yearn for the Sulu Sea.

So I leave. For the Himalayas. To walk among the people, up towards the heavens for days and weeks on end. To decide what to do. For my children I leave gifts to open each day. In small boxes wrapped in handmade paper. Pink with rose petals, sepia with dried seed pods. Each step I take with thinning air, to icy cold clarity. I miss my children, but I feel light and free. I see locals with smiling leathered faces carry scallions and potatoes, chickens and oranges, in baskets on shoulders. Yak dung stacked in neatly spiraled pyramids to dry with heat. I can do this, I can make marriage work, I think. But when I return I know I cannot. I will not pretend for my children. So the kids and I, we leave.

chapter fifty-three

wings

～～～

We get off the plane in Kauai and immediately green gardenia-laden air warms us. Family greets us. White sand creeps into our every crack. It is late July 2015, and school begins in a few days. I have our house reserved in Hanalei, and we can walk to the beach.

We ride bikes with smiles to the rainbow-cradled school. A semester of healing, of return to faint familiarity of youth. Love lavishes here. Freedom and future endless on unguided wanders amidst high sugarcane stalks. Memories of making home with Lucas in abandoned cane factory metal labyrinths, hand in hand, sweet kisses, hands unfettered. Here is where I oiled *Cattle Creek*'s teak decks. Knowing Dad to be at his chart table on the boat, with his sextant, still alive.

Each morning I ride the kids to school on our bikes then ride to the surf beach Pine Trees. There I watch her, hear her waves hum, her depth of life-filled waters and tidal flows. I wrap myself in her caressing wash and ride

her ever-changing waves. Then rest and dry in the sun.
I drink tea on her sands. Like ritual. Innate. Like home.

Dream from my journal:
*I open my wings up on the copper roof of that wildly built
house and the wave of hot air swoops me up and out to
the invisible barrier between the here and now, and there.
The afterlife. I see Dad floating in the air spinning his
arms doing summersaults, smiling, flying, knowing. But
there is a barrier. A crystal-thin bubble veil. Jagged skin
of space and time blurring sound, refracting colour. I
fight to get through it but cannot.*

*I surrender to the air finally after seeing his grin.
Yes, I will see him again in the afterlife. In a ship sailing
in the sky. Where the horizon has even more to share.*

It started with Dad's bedtime stories when I was so young.
His out-of-body experiences. As he gave me back rubs.
Walking his fingers up my spine. Ants, tickles, and spots.
His voice carried me. He tells me he rolled out of his body
on his bed and jaggedly rose to settle, turning facedown,
to spread his wings and hover briefly over my crib. We are
in the tree house he built. A real house perched on a steep
hill and jutting out over the stream below. Supported by
the huge pine tree on the river side. He looks down at me,
feathers rustling, in my crib. My big eyes open and seeing.
He smiles down at me then passes through the wall, into
the crisp evening air, to follow the mist of the riverbed.

Later I dream of perching in the canopies of trees and
taking a leap to fall into the air. Feeling the weight of my
body. The up and down drafts of warm or cool air, always
feeling the weight of my body as my belly might skim the
branches reaching up below me, yet always feeling the rise

of this spirit in me, somehow keeping me buoyant enough to almost get there. Get somewhere.

Sometimes I would perch in old grey barn rafters. With them, the grey spirits, and fly a streak of gold light to every tree carcass I can reach.

And now, I sit on swings in my dreams. That have ropes of long silver braids that I pull this side to turn right, that to turn left—like sails. And I explore up the mountainsides, hidden alpine lakes, finding old rooms of houses I have lived in nestled into rock faces or grass-billowed fields. So much of my life has only been these dreams, and half realities, since I left Dad and *Cattle Creek*.

Like, in my waking sleep, half dreaming on a new moon, I am paralyzed to movement; a dark spirit kneels on my chest with his bony knees and takes away my breath, like a black cat suffocating a baby. He gave me my son and told me to release him. Bring him to the light. So I did. And he shines.

And my daughter, almost two years before, a desolate beach in Baja where the whales swim close and wink at me, she came to be. Her angel wings growing inside of me. There are two red marks on her shoulders where they tore off in my birth canal. But I know they will grow back. And she flies.

Moving to Kauai—the frost, the tension, the pain, the half dream thaws. The dark cloud has lifted. Warmth pours in from every direction and softens me.

I am with family again, in Kauai. My mom, my sisters, their families. And with strong women who reintroduce me to the moon each monthly ceremony. And I feel the healing of the moon cycles. And the moon, she comes back to me, as does my mom, close like they both were in my childhood. My mother takes care of me when I am so sick, my kidney failing. She feeds me miso soup and puts cool rags on my head. After time, the moon comes strong in the breathing meditation, and one night I feel her energy sear the palms of my hands, then settle into the base of my neck, shivering down my spine to my tail-bone, wrapping herself around me with her open wings, opening my heart, my intuition, my arms, to rise, in her guidance, and fly. And also sink again below, to learn. Forgive. And love. Untethered.

chapter fifty-four

breaking free

〰〰〰〰

I have to leave Kauai because I cannot keep the kids from him like this, and we only planned to stay the semester. I know I will be back, but I leave the perfection. In this new awareness, teetering on feeling irresponsible, suspended in space-time, I wonder what is going to give. My heart is so raw. I feel something building. Something in my body though, a physicality, not in my mind, like how it has always been. My mind has stepped back; she observes.

I feel and know that with the opening of my heart after so long, and its subsequent crash, this confused passion has opened the floodgates again forever. I can never go back and protect myself like that, because it shielded everything. The shell drilled open by the octopus beak, held by crushing tentacles, broken, no longer containing the pulsing molten life inside. It is all out. Unfettered desires put forth with honest awareness.

I want to live. I want to feel. Proudly carry this worth. I want a man's loving hands all over me, carrying me. I want to give with no holding back. I want to create. To mother, to love and give my soul. To listen, to learn, to understand. To sing and dance. So I do. And it is so terrifying. Like a broken dam. Where are the filters? Is it okay? How will it be contained? Does it need to be? And will it be? Yes. Because there are the mornings. And because there is the time after the sun sets and before the moon rises when we must sleep. And then there is the body that is superhuman but at times can only handle so much. Energized but also fatigued. There are natural parameters, thank God. And then social parameters . . . which I question more and more, and in questioning celebrate my independence and all my blessings.

And I notice where I feel most comfortable. To whom I feel most drawn. Whom I end up with, or might end up with, as a lover, or fall into friendships with. Which people have stayed in my life and why. Whom my gaze turns to when I travel. I don't always make the easiest choices. I like the risks.

It is that first man who loves women. And I believe him. That I am the only one. It is the woman in a past writing group who writes about how she worked the streets, and encouraged me to investigate my insights with Lee Lee and the girls in the ports. It is the single dad who coaches soccer who has learned life and passion from the streets. It is my friend who is in love after bad relationships, a breakdown—now happily married, with a child. And another, divorced, so strong, always smiling. And the friends who have been there through it all. Even the magical ones who knew me then, with Dad, they are real. Charlie, Gregg, Duncan, Jim and Maria, Amit, Lucas, and so many more. These people I love. With all my bleeding heart.

And I am so naive. Because now I do not have my full shell, just a burgeoning sheath keeping it all together, so magically, so beautifully. I have my intuition. And my past. And the angel. And I learn deep. And I learn hard. And my left arm had been seized closed for years with tense neck and shoulder muscles.

Just before I left Kauai, I met the man who stirred love back into my life, like a witch with a cauldron. I visited again and he massaged my strained, muscled shoulder like a tethered wing, for four hours, four days. And unfurled it. It felt heavy and awkward as I limped around with it. And finally learned to fluff and love and heal it back to rising wingspan billowing, like a spinnaker on a sailboat. But this man tied a string around my ankle, like a boy flying a kite, and watched me fly. And though I am free, I am still wounded in so many ways. He watched me fly until the wind died, or he grew tired, and he watched me, with amusement, crash.

Now I feel vulnerable and beautiful and free. Like we all can be. And this feeling allows me to open my heart after so long. There are kite-flying ones who watch us crash. Waiting. Allowing. He snuck his tentacles around me by asking, after all this other life, twenty years, for me to sail with him, to the Sulu Sea. The witch with a cauldron—he somehow knew it was to ask me back to the sea where I could be queen. By looking at me with those ice blue, so-familiar eyes. By telling me he wanted to marry me. By bringing me swimming to the depths of the ocean in the dark under plankton-glitter spirals. It was surreal. I could not believe it. But I so wanted to believe. Had I manifested this desire in my writing? I had. But I missed some important details. I rushed to my journal and checked.

I had written it only a year before, for my writing class. Now I had to sail on the Sulu Sea. I left my kids with their dad. And this man stirring my heart, talking of marriage and twirling me in the air, we were there together in an old dock in Luzon charting a course right to where Charlie was at gunpoint with the pirates, who are now considered ISIS. And the captain is wild. And there are the same dry-dock girls, or ayam. The boat is cluttered, a home, not tightly organized for survival like *Cattle Creek*. Still, the sailing is magic, the plankton trails still glowing.

But the ocean is not so clean, with smothering oil slicks and floating, bloated fish tangled in swirls of red and blue plastic. And the moonlight drowned by the blaring lighted city of squid boats dredging and destroying the ocean floor, leaving nothing for the local fishermen. And we mostly stay at dock. I realize most sailors do not love the sea as Dad did. They fear the sea. They wait on entire engines or parts or visas for their special girl, for months and months and months instead of staying out of sight of land for weeks like Dad and *Cattle Creek*.

It is familiar to me and feels like home. The markets, the women and their crafts. Sewing sails. I must have opened some rawness in him also, maybe, because it was real, for moments. I trusted him so quickly, I did not even realize it was happening. He is like the octopus who only wants to survive. And we believe and trust as the suction cups caress us, its arms squeeze so subtly tighter. Then leave us curled on the floor in a gelatinous limp of not knowing how to proceed.

And then, we are set free. Because there is no other option. And now I am this shell, this empty, beautiful shell. And I am so empty I can finally feel the spirit that God gave to me, the spirit that is not contained anymore, that can never be contained, filling me. Me. The spirit dances through me, leaving me exhausted, spinning me to laughter, loving me tenderly, teaching me and playing . . . playing . . . playing. It always has.

chapter fifty-five

nowhere to hide

I have always hidden. I mostly hid out of fear. Out of fear that if I expressed that I needed a shower, or food, or sleep, I would be denied. So I bathed, and ate, and slept, in secret. Wherever, however, I could. Never to bring attention to myself.

Then, I hid out of complete inability or lack of knowledge of how to do what I needed to do with support. What if the way I had done things was wrong? And I knew there was something wrong, or different. Like when Dad sent me to that school when I was fourteen, with all girls and nuns and uniforms, after boats and freedom and working girls as friends. The last I ever lived with him. And I washed the dishes at that school. I washed the dishes so discreetly so no one knew I had dirtied them. And the dorm mom appeared and showed me the soap that was under the cabinet that I had dared not open. I felt so ashamed.

And when I could not speak. Or if I did it came out in stutter. Because the pain in my heart and throat would not let it out. It was like sliding the razor-thin edge of my voice over the wounds festering there.

And with my desires. Needing approval, or to be touched, and doing anything, so blindly, to get that. Though always in hiding. Even from my own mind.

And then one day my daughter refuses to take voice lessons. Maybe because I was forcing it on her, because I had wanted someone to make me go to voice lessons, or anything normal like that, when I was her age. And I want to sing out loud. So I take the lesson in her place. But I get somewhere, a C note I think, and I sob. Cry with all the fear in the dark, churning cabin of the boat. The darkness of the port-city streets. The childhood hands and knees on the beer-soaked, spit-dirty barroom floors, the pounding in my ears from the late-night music and drunken talk. The explosions in my head. And the voice teacher helps me heal my voice. Helps me heal my soul. "It is normal," she says. "It is your throat chakra."

And she, with her comforting smile, this music teacher lifts her hand to the sky. Says to me, "C is your root chakra, it is wounded. We will sing through it, in time. In the car just hum there. Or yell there. Or practice staccato and vibrato there. Love on that C in your voice and it will heal."

And it did. And passing that pain swirling in my heart, through the opening of my throat, out into the world. The vibrating, soothing massage of sound. Out it came. My voice. In speech, in words, in awkward foreign scrapings, paintings, and yes, even song. Because of this I find the song circles, medicine of voice, the world, the earth, the roots, meditating in love and light.

I try to heal. The familiar comforts I had sometimes reverted to I no longer want. So I relish her advice, we will sing through it. Now I cannot stop. And it is not always pretty. I have sought help for so long, but did not know for what. And still this need to escape, hide and protect my subsurface, wanting to burst. It is a twisting vine of story blooming and growing. And rotting, incessantly. But I learn from this voice. It is our roots. It is sacred. It is the vine of this life for us all, and it is undeniable and I must embrace it, in the light, in my voice, in my soul.

And where I am now I still love and embrace what is familiar, but no longer hide it. The dark desires we have that I find curious . . . I still ask, is it okay? Or is hiding it what is wrong? Is so many years of repression, suppression, hanging of witches, denying bacchanalian baths, sacrifices to gods and goddesses okay? Is fear and egos and power to squash right? Those things are not okay.

But our desires are beautiful. It is how we survive. And where is the balance? That is this life. That is our dance, our song. To feel this inner thing fuel us, then nurture it with care and open it out into the world for everyone to see and love.

But there will always be secrets. Parts to hold back. Some we may not even realize. A hidden germination. Like a seed deep under the earth with the worms and fecal fertility. It is private. And it will blossom into beauty. Like death. Like life. Not to hide from, but to veil with a delicate shell when appropriate, then reach into the sun with petals of crimson to admire, with sweet dew to draw the bees to spread the seemingly impossible result of miraculous strength and life.

chapter fifty-six

impermanence

~~~~~~~~

I had no choice but to face what I had always been hiding from. Because I finally hiked into the swamp to meet her, this monster inside that I ran from. She is beautiful and ugly. She rages and is calm. She is everything I have felt under the surface all these years, and now I understand, and I love her. Her darkness is what makes her light unique. The individual pulsing energy in this mass of timelessness.

The smell of her is of the sea. But with a tinge of earth. The saline mist. The hot dry dirt after it is saturated with rain. Ylang-ylang flower oil. Sometimes she smells of sage and cigarette smoke on the breath.

She can take things away anytime she wants. Basic things, like sleep, like fresh water to drink, like warmth and home. Like love. Like life. Or she can give too much. Like pleasure. And watch as you don't know how to moderate. Then she can take it away again, completely.

That is why I am afraid to have a home. Because I build them, like my dad did. Beautiful with huge windows opening to the mountain, or the ocean. The horizon that we reach for so clearly in our view. Houses built with wood from the old redwood barn, or teak from part of our boat. Or tiles my grandfather made. The construction is the fun.

But something always happens. Love gets complicated and my mom leaves, because what else could she do? Speeding down the dirt road to make a plume of dust. A home is not the same without a mom. Even though there were tears and screaming from confusion and pain. It is not the same. And Dad dies, so that home, we leave also. And I never make it to that home in Switzerland, so it is also gone.

But I leave that next house. Just like the last. It becomes my pattern. And I try to do something different, to fix it by basing a home on love. First I run away because I am afraid I don't know how to manage what is inside me. I do not trust his beautiful mind, his athletic body, because I do not know how and I still hide so much. That house sat for a moment suspended in time, sparsely decorated with carvings from the Sulu Sea and tapestries from Africa. With the wooden table that belonged to my grandparents and holds the space, like a home should, for dinner parties with the friends who stay, no matter where I move.

And then the home for babies with cherry trees and the rushing stream. By then, I had forgotten how to love, and my blind passion grew the seeds of life within me. With a man who had also forgotten how to love, because someone sped away from him also, because we had known those who were afraid to love and repeated the fear. And kids need love, not fear. The windows look out to the mountain, and the heavy, beautiful storm clouds, and we leave.

And always to the ocean, a moving home, always there. Our boat from childhood and youth, I yearn to get back to. That is where I want to go, even though that is where she resides, when she does not visit me. Her seaweed tentacles lure me, sometimes want to pull me, with the help of the dark-night crashing wave, down to the depths of the blue.

And another attempt to save love. To build the home in the mountains. Large, light spaces, flowing breeze, wildflowers blooming and elk feasting on spring grass. But it is cold there. The winter too long. The ice crystals grow before my eyes on those ceiling-high windows. The snowflake octagons reach arms spreading white. Reaching icy blue so intricate in detail, so mesmerizing up close as I watch it grow, it is encasing me inside.

She sneaks her tentacle in and rescues me. Slithers her warm seawater suction cups around my ankle and gently yanks.

But her yank has always been of love, and she pulls me home, to Kauai, where I have no home in my many homes. Where I thought I found love and we began to build a house of bamboo, and I finish building it, alone. But she embraces me. I finally see the green-gold of her eyes. I feel her intoxication of mother forcing me to find the love within myself. She teaches me love has no home; it is everywhere.

Our children teach us this also. They make us good at love no matter how hard we try to run from it. They soften their dad and teach him to love them. And my mom returns. She and my sisters live on the same island with us. With years of perspective, I finally see Mom's pain. She is graceful and so intelligent, and still silly and lovely. And I am grateful that we share days together, that my children know their nana. They can touch her skin, feel the expressions of her face, know the golden magic in her eyes.

So now, this sea monster within myself, can love herself. She can love her children, a man, have a home, with her now-dark roots still reaching through the earth, who bursts forth her natural gifts, still some green shoots, but ultimately to the ocean and up to the sun. To create. To provide. To care. Heal the fear. The walls calcify slowly, delicately. And the inside oozes in and out, reaching to blindly suction a new territory. Home might be messy with seaweed and shells, and orchids and sage, and red muddy footprints, moist sheets. But I want to clean it, and love it, each day. To allow more mess. To allow the pain. Because I can no longer hide. It is not possible. And that is when love stays.

Yacht, *Cattle Creek*

about the author

Rebecca Stirling lives between Aspen, Colorado, and Kauai, Hawaii, with her two children. She teaches creative art and writing classes to help spread the knowledge and ingenuity of world cultures. She continues to sail and travel, read and write, and has a love for the stories individuals, cultures, and our earth have to tell.

SELECTED TITLES FROM SHE WRITES PRESS

She Writes Press is an independent publishing ompany founded to serve women writers everywhere. Visit us at www.shewritespress.com.

Fourteen: A Daughter's Memoir of Adventure, Sailing, and Survival by Leslie Johansen Nack. $16.95, 978-1-63152-941-2. A coming-of-age adventure story about a young girl who comes into her own power, fights back against abuse, becomes an accomplished sailor, and falls in love with the ocean and the natural world.

Naked Mountain: A Memoir by Marcia Mabee. $16.95, 978-1-63152-097-6. A compelling memoir of one woman's journey of natural world discovery, tragedy, and the enduring bonds of marriage, set against the backdrop of a stunning mountaintop in rural Virginia.

The Sportscaster's Daughter: A Memoir by Cindi Michael. $16.95, 978-1-63152-107-2. Despite being disowned by her father—sportscaster George Michael, said to be the man who inspired ESPN's SportsCenter—Cindi Michael manages financially and heals emotionally, ultimately finding confidence from within.

Seeing Red: A Woman's Quest for Truth, Power, and the Sacred by Lone Morch. $16.95, 978-1-938314-12-4. One woman's journey over inner and outer mountains—a quest that takes her to the holy Mt. Kailas in Tibet, through a seven-year marriage, and into the arms of the fierce goddess Kali, where she discovers her powerful, feminine self.

Singing with the Sirens: Overcoming the Long-Term Effects of Childhood Sexual Exploitation by Ellyn Bell and Stacey Bell. $16.95, 978-1-63152-936-8. With metaphors of sea creatures and the force of the ocean as a backdrop, this work addresses the problems of sexual abuse and exploitation of young girls, taking the reader on a poetic journey toward finding healing from within.

Secrets in Big Sky Country: A Memoir by Mandy Smith. $16.95, 978-1-63152-814-9. A bold and unvarnished memoir about the shattering consequences of familial sexual abuse—and the strength it takes to overcome them.